CELEBRATE 2000!
Reflections on God the Father

Celebrate 2000!

Reflections on God the Father
WITH QUESTIONS FOR REFLECTION
AND DISCUSSION

POPE JOHN PAUL II

Selected and Arranged by
Paul Thigpen, Ph.D.

CHARIS
SERVANT PUBLICATIONS
ANN ARBOR, MICHIGAN

Charis Books is an imprint of Servant Publications especially designed to serve
Roman Catholics.

All selections have been taken from the official Vatican translation of papal
documents. Some are from encyclicals and apostolic letters published in the
United States by Pauline Books & Media. Other texts appeared originally in the
official Vatican newspaper, *L'Osservatore Romano* (English edition, Via del
Pellegrino, 00120 Vatican City, Europe). They were reprinted in *The Pope
Speaks,* a bimonthly periodical published by *Our Sunday Visitor* (200 Noll Plaza,
Huntington, IN 46750). Used by permission. All rights reserved.

Published by Servant Publications
P.O. Box 8617
Ann Arbor, Michigan 48107

Cover photo: © Corbis/Bettmann. Used by permission.

98 99 00 01 10 9 8 7 6 5 4 3 2

Printed in the United States of America
ISBN 1-56955-077-8

LIBRARY OF CONGRESS CATALOGING-IN-PUBLICATION DATA

John Paul II, 1920–
Celebrate 2000! : reflections on God the Father : weekly readings for 1999 /
Pope John Paul II : selected and arranged by Paul Thigpen.
    p.   cm. —(Celebrate 2000! series)
Includes bibliographical references.
ISBN 1-56955-077-8 (alk. paper)
1. God—Fatherhood—Papal teachings. 2. Catholic Church—Doctrines—
Papal teachings. 3. Devotional calendars—Catholic Church. I. Thigpen,
Thomas Paul, 1954–   . II. Title. III. Series.
BT153.F3J64   1998
242'.2—dc21   98-5143
                                                                          CIP

CONTENTS

Before We Can Celebrate,
We Have To Meditate

As the new millennium approaches, prophecies of doomsday grow increasingly shrill. Yet in the midst of these troubled and troubling voices, a calmer, more optimistic voice calls out to focus attention on the year 2000. While others cry, "Repent— for the end is near," Pope John Paul II declares, "Repent— for a new beginning has come!" While some prepare for disaster, he calls the Church and indeed the whole world to prepare instead for the third millennium, with a burning hope that God the Father, through Christ and His Spirit, is still at work to renew His beloved creation.

The future, insists the Pope, holds remarkable possibilities for those who open themselves to the Holy Spirit's intentions. The year 2000 is actually a door of divine grace. If we will cross this "threshold of hope" into God's purposes, he says, we can take part in a "new springtime" that heralds the transformation of ourselves, our Church, our nation, and our entire planet.

Confident in this hope, Pope John Paul has announced that the Church will observe the year 2000 as a "Great Jubilee": a particular year of God's favor, a sign of His unfailing love, a season to remember and rejoice that two millennia ago, Christ came to set us free from the bonds of sin. Like all Jubilee years, it will be, he says, "a year of the remission of sins and of the punishments due them, a year of reconciliation between disputing parties, a year of manifold conversions and of sacramental and extra-sacramental penance." The Pope wants the entire year to be celebrated exuberantly as an unprecedented birthday party for Jesus—and the whole world is invited to come.

But we can't show up at a birthday party dirty-faced, ragged, and empty-handed. We have to get ourselves ready to honor the Lord and to celebrate His coming. No doubt our heavenly Father loves us as we are, spiritual urchins though we may be. Yet He loves us too much to let us remain as we are. For that reason, the Pope calls us to make preparations.

The whole Christian community should enjoy the Great Jubilee as a feast that will nourish our spirits, put a song in our hearts, and send us out into the world dancing. Before that can happen for most of us, however, we have some work to do. It's time to give our souls a bath, to dress in our spiritual best, and to take in our hands the gift of our will, wrapped in a fervent desire to see Christ's kingdom come.

To help us get ready for this grand party, Pope John Paul outlined a strategy in his Apostolic Letter of November 10, 1994, entitled "The Coming Third Millennium." There, he noted that the Second

Vatican Council, subsequent church synods, holy years, and papal teachings have all played their part in moving the Church toward the Jubilee. But in these last few years of the fading second millennium, the Church needs a specific program of practical initiatives designed to prepare us for the dawning third millennium.

The Holy Father called for special preparations in the years 1997, 1998, and 1999 that are intended to turn the Church's attention to God Himself, to help us grow deeper in our knowledge of Him, our love for Him, our joy in Him. Each of these years he asked to be devoted to reflection on a particular Person within the Holy Trinity: Father, Son, and Holy Spirit.

The order in which he called us to meditate on the three Persons of God in these years reflects, at least in one sense, the order in which we encounter them in human history and in our personal lives. The first year, 1997, was intended to center on God the Son, Jesus Christ—the One whose glorious invasion of history and of our lives first allowed us to encounter God face-to-face. In 1998, we turned our attention to God the Holy Spirit, Love Himself, the Person sent by Christ to set ablaze the hearts of His disciples and, by their hands, to turn the world upside down. In the Spirit's coming at Pentecost, the Church has encountered God as the One who lives in us and through us.

Finally, in the year 1999, we must focus on God the Father. The Son of God and the Spirit of God came precisely for this reason: to turn our hearts toward the Father, to restore our friendship with Him, to bring us back to His loving embrace. We center on Him in this last year because He Himself is our final destination, the One we will encounter at last as the source of all things and the fulfillment of all things.

In each year, Pope John Paul suggests, we should allow our meditation on a Person of the Holy Trinity to lead us to reflect as well on certain related themes. Faith, hope, and love—the three "theological virtues," as they have been called—provide one such set of themes. As we turn our souls toward Christ, we should ponder the meaning of faith in Him. As we look to the Holy Spirit, we should dwell on the meaning of the hope He brings. And as we seek out God the Father, who loved the world into being, we should delve deeply into the meaning of this love.

The Holy Father goes on to note that other themes fall naturally into the focus of meditation for each of the three years. Concerns about ecumenism, for example, easily arise when we begin to think of Christ and of all those who call themselves by His name. Thoughts about the nature of the Church accompany thoughts about the Holy Spirit, who fills and energizes the Church. Reflection on God the Father, who created all people, presses us to consider as well our role in serving the world beyond the Church.

Finally, in his apostolic letter the Pope calls all Christians to take part in the Jubilee preparations.

"Everyone," he urges, "is asked to do as much as possible to ensure that the great challenge of the Year 2000 is not overlooked, for this challenge certainly involves a special grace of the Lord for the Church and for the whole of humanity." This book is an effort to heed that call, to make some small contribution to the Church's preparation for that year of divine favor. For what better way could there be to encourage God's people to nourish themselves on these vital themes than to offer Pope John Paul's own profound reflections as food for thought?

The structure of this book, which is a compilation of brief excerpts from the Holy Father's extensive written works, follows his strategy for preparation. As a collection of readings with study questions for the year 1999, it centers on God the Father, on the virtue of love, on Mary as a model of love, and on associated topics such as sin, conversion and penance; Christian social and political responsibility; the family; the sanctity of life; and interreligious dialogue.

The goal here, of course, is not simply meditation, but transformation. The Pope has called us to look long and hard at God because to know God truly is to love Him, and to love Him truly is to become like Him. St. Paul spoke of the process long ago: "We all,...beholding the glory of the Lord, are being changed into his likeness" (2 Cor 3:18 RSV). St. John promised that "we shall be like [God]" when we "see Him as He is"; and even the hope of seeing Him purifies us (see 1 Jn 3:2-3). In setting our minds on the Lord during these three years, then, we're bathing and dressing our souls, getting ready for Jesus' grand birthday party, where the gift we bring will be ourselves.

Several important concerns have shaped my choice of study questions. First, because I want to encourage a careful reading of what the Holy Father has said, some questions simply require the reader to go back to the text in order to search out a key thought he has made explicit. Other questions, however, point beyond the text to the ideas implicit there—to the critical assumptions or the definitions of significant terms that form the foundation for the meaning of the text.

I've decided, after some deliberation, to pose most of the questions in the first person singular. That is to say, instead of asking the reader, "What does this mean to you and what must you do about it?" this study guide has each person ask him- or herself: "What does this mean to *me* and what must *I* do about it?" Such an approach, I think, presses the reader to respond in some personal, immediate way to what the Holy Father has said.

Why not the first person plural—"we" instead of "I"? No doubt the frequent occurrence of "I" and "me" in the questions could be mistaken as a kind of narrowness or self-centeredness, a neglect of the "we." Yet in many cases *we* cannot get very far in making a difference in the world if there hasn't first been a change in *me*.

The questions here reflect a mix of the theoretical and the practical, the theological and the pastoral, but the emphasis is decidedly on the practical and pastoral. Repeatedly the reader is urged to consider the specific, concrete ways in which he or she can act on the Holy Father's insights. What good, for example, does it accomplish to meditate on the Christian's role in the workplace if I don't go on to identify and address the concrete problems that need resolution in my particular place of employment?

Finally, readers will note soon enough that the purpose of these questions is not to challenge the Holy Father, to submit him to a critique, or to provide opportunity for a Church-wide referendum on what he has to say. He already has more than enough critics who busy themselves with such work. These meditations were of course not issued as infallible papal pronouncements, so Catholics aren't under any obligation to agree with them all. Nevertheless, I've chosen precisely these particular excerpts from the vast body of his writings because I'm convinced that in them he forcefully challenges *us* and submits *our* lives to a piercing critique. We can ignore what he has to say only at great peril to ourselves, to the Church, and to the world.

Despite that peril, I look with hope to God our Father, who is Himself "the God of hope" [Rom 15:13

NAB], to open our ears and our hearts as we continue in our journey home to Him. With John Paul, we can look eagerly to the new millennium—and celebrate with confidence the coming "springtime for the Gospel."

Paul Thigpen

How to Use This Book

The structure of this book, which is a compilation of brief excerpts from the Holy Father's extensive written works, follows his strategy for preparation. This collection of readings with study questions for the year 1999, centers on God the Father, on the virtue of love, on Mary as a model of love, and on associated topics such as the importance of family, our call to social justice, and the gift of the human conscience.

The goal here, of course, is not simply meditation, but transformation. The Pope has called us to look long and hard at God because to know God truly is to love Him, and to love Him truly is to become like Him. St. Paul spoke of the process long ago: "We all,… beholding the glory of the Lord, are being changed into his likeness" (2 Cor 3:18, RSV). St. John promised that "we shall be like [God]" when we "see Him as He is"; and even the hope of seeing Him purifies us (see 1 Jn 3:2-3). In setting our minds on the Lord during these three years, then, we're bathing and dressing our souls, getting ready for Jesus' grand birthday party, where the gift we bring will be ourselves.

Several important concerns have shaped my choice of study questions. First, because I want to encourage a careful reading of what the Holy Father has said, some questions simply require the reader to go back to the text in order to search out a key thought he has made explicit. Other questions, however, point beyond the text to the ideas implicit there—to the critical assumptions or the definitions of significant terms that form the foundation for the meaning of the text.

I've decided, after some deliberation, to pose most of the questions in the first person singular. That is to say, instead of asking the reader, "What does this mean to you and what must you do about it?" this study guide has each person ask him- or herself: "What does this mean to *me* and what must *I* do about it?" Such an approach, I think, presses the reader to respond in some personal, immediate way to what the Holy Father has said.

Why not the first person plural—"we" instead of "I"? No doubt the frequent occurrence of "I" and "me" in the questions could be mistaken as a kind of narrowness or self-centeredness, a neglect of the "we." Yet in many cases *we* cannot get very far in making a difference in the world if there hasn't first been a change in *me.*

The questions here reflect a mix of the theoretical and the practical, the theological and the pastoral, but the emphasis is decidedly on the practical and pastoral. Repeatedly the reader is urged to consider the specific, concrete ways in which he or she can act on the Holy Father's insights. What good, for example, does it accomplish to meditate on the Church's role as a "sacrament of reconciliation" if I don't go on to identify and approach those individuals in my life with whom I need to be reconciled?

Finally, readers will note soon enough that the purpose of these questions is not to challenge the Holy Father, to submit him to a critique, or to provide opportunity for a Church-wide referendum on what he has to say. He already has more than enough critics who busy themselves with such work. These meditations were of course not issued as infallible papal pronouncements, so Catholics aren't under any obligation to agree with them all. Nevertheless, I've chosen precisely these particular excerpts from the vast body of his writings because I'm convinced that in them he forcefully challenges *us* and submits *our* lives to a piercing critique. We can ignore what he has to say only at great peril to ourselves, to the Church, and to the world.

Despite that peril, I place my hope firmly in the Father who love us, trusting him" to open our ears and our hearts. With the Holy Father himself, we can look eagerly to the new millennium—and celebrate with confidence the coming "springtime for the Gospel."

—Paul Thigpen

Personal Reflection Questions

OUR FATHER, WHO ART IN HEAVEN

1. A Pilgrimage to the Father's House
   - In which areas of my life do I need a "broadening of horizons" in order to see things from God's perspective?
   - To be on a "great pilgrimage to the house of the Father" implies movement and change throughout the Christian life; what kinds of movement and change are needed in my life just now if I am to move closer to God?

2. God the Father Is Love
   - In what specific ways have I abused the freedom God gave me by rejecting Him, disobeying Him, opposing Him, or treating Him "like a rival"?
   - How has "refusal of God's fatherly love and loving gifts" led to division, isolation, and polarization among various groups in our society?

3. The Father of Mercy
   - What is keeping me from seeking forgiveness from "the Father of mercy" just now—pride? fear? doubt? confusion?
   - If to see Jesus is to see the Father [see Jn 14:9], what specific attributes and actions of

Jesus in the Gospels that reflect His character should encourage us to turn to the Father?

THE VIRTUE OF LOVE

4.   Man, the Image of the God Who Is Love
   - What exactly does it mean to say that human beings are made "in the image and likeness of God"?
   - What would it mean for me to demonstrate a "true openness to [my] fellow human beings and solidarity with them" in my community?

5.   Imitate Jesus' Love
   - In order to imitate Jesus, am I willing to ask in every situation, "What would Jesus do?"—and then do it?
   - In what circumstances have I found it to be true that love must be more than a precept— that it must be a gift of grace from God that goes beyond my own abilities?

MARY, MODEL OF LOVE

6.   A Mother's Inexhaustible Love
   - How has Mary expressed her motherly love for the Church and the world, both during her life on earth and since her assumption into heaven?
   - In what ways does "the Father's eternal love" come "close to each of us" through Mary?

7.   Mary's Loving and Urgent Invitation
   • Mary made herself God's servant, "the hand-maid of the Lord"; in what ways today can I imitate her loving servanthood to God and the people around me?
   • Mary says to me, "Do whatever Christ tells you"; what has He told me to do that I haven't yet done?

SIN, CONVERSION, PENANCE AND MERCY

8.   Acknowledging Our Sin
   • In what ways have I been tempted to view God as "an enemy," a "source of danger and threat," a "limitation" of myself—rather than as the source of my own freedom and "the fullness of good"?
   • If "it is not possible to deal with sin and conversion only in abstract terms," in what concrete ways must I deal with the issue here and now so that I can continue "on the road of return to the Father"?

9.   Sin, a Wounding of the Church
   • How does even the most private, most hidden of my personal sins ultimately result in a wounding of the Church?
   • Why does a full reconciliation with God always involve, at least implicitly, a reconciliation with His Church?

10. A Proper Sense of Sin
    - In what areas have I allowed my conscience to be "eclipsed" so that I have lost "a healthy awareness" of my own sinfulness?
    - Have I bought into the popular definition of happiness as a matter of "satisfying oneself and being satisfied with oneself"?

11. The Twofold Injury of Sin
    - Why is every sin ultimately a "suicidal act"?
    - Which of my sins have I been tempted to blame on external factors (circumstances, events, other individuals, society as a whole) as a way of attempting to avoid responsibility for my actions?

12. The Human Conscience
    - Why is my conscience not an infallible guide to right and wrong?
    - In what specific ways can I nurture and educate my conscience so that it will be more closely conformed to objective truth and to God's law?

13. Are We Repentant or Self-Satisfied?
    - Am I more like the Pharisee or the tax collector in Jesus' parable?
    - Are there any ethical issues in which I am trying to adapt the moral norm to my own "capacities and personal interests" or in which I am attempting to reject the idea of a moral norm altogether?

14. Mary, the Model of the Moral Life
    - Why is the making of excuses for people's sin only a counterfeit love rather than a genuine love?
    - Why does the attempt to justify our sin empty Christ's sacrifice of its power in our lives?

15. Conversion and Penance
    - Do I resist the notion that I should accept and carry out certain sacrifices as a way of correcting the sin in my life?
    - Am I making sacramental Confession regularly enough and sincerely enough so that it increases the sensitivity of my conscience, purifies me more deeply, instills me with peace, and helps me resist temptation and strive for a life closer to God?

16. The Individual Aspect of Penance
    - Why can individual penance never be replaced by communal penance?
    - When I make a sacramental Confession, what steps can I take to make sure that I confess my sins "with the whole depth of [my] conscience and with the whole of [my] sense of guilt and of trust in God"?

17. Penance, Channel of Redemptive Power
    - Have I claimed to receive forgiveness while disregarding the very "Sacrament instituted by Christ precisely for forgiveness"?
    - How does the confessional become the birth-

place, not only of a "new, uncontaminated ... reconciled individual," but also of "a reconciled world"?

18. The Triumph of Mercy
   • Am I ever tempted to despair that my sin is powerful enough to erase God's mercy?
   • Have I nurtured a confidence in God's mercy that keeps me coming back regularly to the confessional despite my failings?

CHRISTIAN MORAL RESPONSIBILITY

19. The Church Must Acknowledge Past Sins
   • How have I "indulged in ways of thinking and acting that were truly forms of counterwitness and scandal" rather than a testimony to Christ?
   • To what extent have I "been shaped by the climate of secularism and ethical relativism"?

20. Clear Moral Teaching Is Liberating
   • Why does moral confusion result from educational theories which propose that people must create their own values, and that feeling good about themselves is a primary moral principle?
   • When Christian morality sometimes seems to me "too demanding, difficult to understand, and almost impossible to practice," do I remember to look to Jesus with the simple desire to be united more fully to Him?

THE FAMILY

21. Marriage, Sign of Christ's Love for the Church
    - Why is sexual love alone an insufficient basis for the marriage union?
    - In what concrete ways can the conjugal life be "a way of holiness for Christian spouses"?

22. An Indissoluble Communion
    - Why is it more critical than ever that the Church strongly reaffirm the reality that marriage is indissoluble?
    - How can my personal faithfulness—either through fidelity in marriage or chastity in singleness—serve as a "small and precious sign" of God's faithfulness to us all?

23. The Trials of Marriage Can Be Redemptive
    - How can a couple's marriage trials "strengthen their union and lead them to a greater joy"?
    - What does it mean to say that in marriage as in all of the Christian life, "redemption is tied to the Cross"?

24. Marriage and Virginity or Celibacy
    - How do the two vocations of marriage and consecrated virginity or celibacy each affirm, support and enhance the meaning of the other?
    - How does the commitment to celibacy of single persons strengthen the fidelity of married couples?

25. The Sovereignty of the Family
    - In what ways is the family the "primordial" and "sovereign" society?
    - Is there someone I know who needs my loving concern because he or she has a broken family or no family at all?

26. Spiritual Formation in the Family
    - If I am a parent, am I carrying out the kind of catechetical instruction of my children that is natural and appropriate for the "domestic Church" that is in my home?
    - If I am not a parent, how can I support the parents I know in the spiritual formation of their families?

27. Family Prayer
    - Am I regularly taking advantage of "suitable moments" for personal or family prayer that help to consecrate daily life in my home?
    - Do I give my children and others an encouraging example of living "in personal dialogue" with God?

28. Honor Within the Family
    - How does honoring one another in the home serve as the "safeguard" of the family?
    - What specific steps can I take to show honor to my parents, my children and my siblings?

29. The Roles of Father and Mother
    - What "profound ... effects" does the quality of the relationship between spouses have on their children?

- In our culture, what are the most common ways in which parents are tempted to leave a damaging absence or exert an "oppressive presence" in the lives of their children?

30. The Work of Mothers
   - In my workplace, is labor structured in such a way that "women do not have to pay for their advancement" at the expense of their families?
   - How could our society make it easier for a mother to care for her children "without inhibiting her freedom, without psychological or practical discrimination, and without penalizing her as compared with other women"?

31. The Role of Children
   - What is the "active role that little ones have in the Kingdom of God"?
   - In what specific ways do I need to change so as to become like a child, as Jesus insisted?

32. Youth Need a High Moral Vision
   - What young people might be looking to me for guidance or an example, and in what practical ways can I help instill in them a high moral vision?
   - What are the perils of an educational system "without a value system based on truth"?

33. The Special Role of Older People
   - What concrete opportunities in the apostolate are open to older people in my parish and community?
   - How can I help the older people I know with

health problems or other physical limitations more closely identify with the sufferings and weakness of Christ?

WOMEN

34. The Church Is Grateful for Women
    - What "manifestations of the feminine genius" throughout Church history have most inspired me to imitation as a disciple of Jesus?
    - For what "fruits of feminine holiness" among the women I know am I most grateful?

35. Advancing the Dignity of Women
    - Is there any way, however subtle, in which I have contributed to the common mentality that women should be viewed as commodities or as instruments of pleasure?
    - How can women in the Scriptures serve as models for women's lives today?

36. Special Tasks Entrusted to Women
    - How can women work to bring "full dignity to the conjugal life and to motherhood"?
    - How can women assure "the moral dimension of culture"?

CHRISTIAN SOCIAL ACTION

37. Caring for Those Most in Need
    - What does the Church mean by "the option or love of preference for the poor"?

- How do I go about reconciling the "valid and necessary" right to private property with the Christian social principle that "the goods of this world are originally meant for all"?

38. No Reconciliation Without Conversion
   - Why must reconciliation between peoples be rooted in a deep internal conversion that rejects sin at its roots?
   - How, in my everyday circumstances, might I personally contribute to "changing a historical condition of hatred and violence into a civilization of love"?

THE SPHERES OF HUMAN LIFE: POLITICS, ECONOMICS, CULTURE, SCIENCE

39. Charity and Justice in Public Life
   - Why can charity never be separated from justice?
   - What excuses have I offered for failing to be actively involved in public life?

40. The Christian in Politics
   - What are the "Gospel values" intimately connected with political service?
   - Why must we always keep in mind as we labor to improve society that no political system is perfect?

41. The Christian in the Workplace
   - In addition to mere profits, what "human and

moral factors" must be considered in evaluating the health of a business?

- How should I seek to resist the "idolatry of the market" as I encounter it in my own workplace?

42. The Christian in Culture
    - What elements now "critically burden" our culture and need "purification" through "courage and intellectual creativity in the privileged places of culture"?
    - How can I allow the gospel to permeate more deeply my "thought patterns, standards of judgement, and norms of behavior"?

43. Science, Faith, and the World's Future
    - Why is the dialogue between science and faith "doubly necessary" in the development and application of technology?
    - In what current areas of scientific research and development is there a critical danger that scientists might neglect or avoid the ethical implications of their work?

44. Respect for Creation
    - What limits has God placed on humankind's "dominion" over the rest of creation?
    - What specific considerations about the moral dimensions of "development" must we keep in mind in our stewardship of the world?

WITNESSES TO THE GOSPEL OF LIFE

45.   The Worth of the Human Person
    • Why do we not have the moral authority to do with human life whatever we will?
    • What critical social and political issues demand my efforts to assure that the sacredness of all human life will be respected?

46.   Abortion, an Unspeakable Crime
    • Has fear of hostility from my peers made me succumb to the use of ambiguous terminology in reference to abortion in such a way that its true nature and seriousness is hidden?
    • Am I willing to recognize and act on the reality that when we deal with abortion, "we are dealing with murder"?

47. Defend Life!
    • If the ultimate test of a nation's greatness is the way we treat "the weakest and most defenseless" among us, what is the present moral and spiritual condition of our nation?
    • Why does every other "great cause" of humanity lose its meaning when we fail to guarantee the right to life?

INTERRELIGIOUS DIALOGUE

48.   Part of the Church's Evangelizing Mission
    • Why must dialogue with people of other religions be carried out alongside evangelization without confusing the two?

31

- Why must interreligious dialogue be conducted "with the conviction that the Church is the ordinary means of salvation and that she alone possesses the fullness of the means of salvation"?

49. Dialogue Based on Respect, Hope, and Love
    - How do other religions challenge the Church to discover and acknowledge Christ's presence and the Spirit's work throughout the world; to examine more deeply her own identity; and to bear witness to the fullness of God's revelation in Christ?
    - How might a misdirected interreligious dialogue lead to "abandonment of principles" or a "false irenicism"?

WORKING FOR PEACE

50. Building Peace
    - Why are Christians especially obliged to work for peace in the world?
    - Why is prayer "*par excellence* the power needed" to achieve peace in the world?

51. Peace and Justice
    - On what "essential human values" is peace based?
    - Why does the denial of justice lead to the loss of peace?

52. Peace Is Possible
   - Why can we dare to hope that peace is possible?
   - If peace is my "grave duty," what specific steps am I taking to work for it?

1999

YEAR THREE OF PREPARATION:
Weekly Readings on God the Father

Our Father, Who Art In Heaven

God the Father loved the world into being. Though the world has spurned Him, He has sent the Son and the Spirit to call the world back into His loving embrace. As the Father is our beginning, He must also become our destination.

THE WEEK OF JANUARY 3, 1999

1. A Pilgrimage to the Father's House

The third and final year of preparation will be aimed at broadening the horizons of believers, so that they will see things in the perspective of Christ: in the perspective of the "Father who is in heaven" (see Matthew 5:45), from whom the Lord was sent and to whom He has returned (see John 16:28).

"This is eternal life, that they know you the only true God, and Jesus Christ whom you have sent" (see John 17:3). The whole of the Christian life is like a great pilgrimage to the house of the Father, whose unconditional love for every human creature, and in particular for the "prodigal son" (see Luke 15:11-32), we discover anew each day. This pilgrimage takes place in the heart of each person, extends to the believing community, and then reaches to the whole of humanity.

The Jubilee, centered on the person of Christ, thus becomes a great act of praise to the Father: "Blessed be the God and Father of our Lord Jesus Christ, who has blessed us in Christ with every spiritual blessing in the heavenly places, even as he chose us in him before the foundation of the world, that we should be holy and blameless before him" (Eph 1:3-4, RSV). [TMA n. 49]

2. GOD THE FATHER IS LOVE

The Church, as a reconciled and reconciling community, cannot forget that at the source of her gift and mission of reconciliation is the initiative, full of compassionate love and mercy, of that God who is love (see 1 John 4:8) and who out of love created human beings (see Wisdom 11:23-26; Genesis 1:27; Psalms 8:4-8)....
He created them so that they might live in friendship with Him and in communion with one another.

God is faithful to His eternal plan even when man, under the impulse of the evil one (see Wisdom 2:24) and carried away by his own pride, abuses the freedom given to him in order to love and generously seek what is good, and [instead] refuses to obey his Lord and Father. God is faithful even when man, instead of responding with love to God's love, opposes Him and treats Him like a rival, deluding himself and relying on his own power, with the resulting break of relationship with the One who created him. In spite of this transgression on man's part, God remains faithful in love.

It is certainly true that the story of the Garden of Eden makes us think about the tragic consequences of rejecting the Father, which becomes evident in man's inner disorder and in the breakdown of harmony between man and woman, brother and brother (see Genesis 3:12ff; 4:1-16). Also significant is the Gospel parable of the two brothers (the parable of the "prodigal son"; see Luke 15:11-32) who, in different ways, distance themselves from their father and cause a rift between them. Refusal of God's fatherly love and of His loving gifts is always at the root of humanity's divisions.

But we know that God, "rich in mercy" (Eph 2:4), like the father in the parable [of the prodigal son], does not close His heart to any of His children. He waits for them, looks for them, goes to meet them at the place where the refusal of communion imprisons them in isolation and division. He calls them to gather about His table in the joy of the feast of forgiveness and reconciliation.

This initiative on God's part is made concrete and manifest in the redemptive act of Christ, which radiates through the world by means of the ministry of the Church. [RP n. 10]

3. THE FATHER OF MERCY

Revelation and faith teach us not only to meditate in the abstract upon the mystery of God as "Father of mercies," but also to have recourse to that mercy in the name of Christ and in union with Him. Did not Christ say that our Father, who "sees in secret" (Mt 6:4, 6, 18), is always waiting for us to have recourse to Him in every need and always waiting for us to study His mystery—the mystery of the Father and His love? (see Ephesians 3:18, Luke 11:5-13)....

Although God "dwells in unapproachable light" (1 Tm 6:16, RSV), He speaks to man by means of the whole of the universe: "ever since the creation of the world his invisible nature, namely, His eternal power and deity, has been clearly perceived in the things that have been made" (Rom 1:20). This indirect and imperfect knowledge, achieved by the intellect seeking God by means of creatures through the visible world, [nevertheless] falls short of [a] vision of the

Father. "No one has ever seen God," writes St. John, in order to stress the truth that "the only Son, who is in the bosom of the Father, He has made Him known" (Jn 1:18).

This "making known" [of the Father by Christ] reveals God in the most profound mystery of His being, one and three, surrounded by "unapproachable light...." Through this "making known" by Christ, we know God above all in His relationship of love for man.... It is precisely here that "His invisible nature" becomes in a special way "visible," incomparably more visible than through all the other "things that have been made": it becomes visible in Christ and through Christ, through His actions and His words, and finally through His death on the Cross and His resurrection. [DM n. 2]

THE VIRTUE OF LOVE

The Father has created us out of the superabundance of his love, and "whoever loves is born of God and knows God" (see 1 John 4:7).

THE WEEK OF JANUARY 24, 1999

4. MAN, THE IMAGE OF THE GOD WHO IS LOVE

God created man in His own image and likeness (see Genesis 1:26-27): Calling him to existence through love, He called him at the same time for love.

God is love (see 1 John 4:8) and in Himself He lives a mystery of personal loving communion. Creating the human race in His own image and continually keeping it in being, God inscribed in the humanity of man and woman the vocation, and thus the capacity and responsibility, of love and communion. Love is therefore the fundamental and innate vocation of every human being. [FC n. 11]

The vocation to love, understood as true openness to our fellow human beings and solidarity with them, is the most basic of all vocations. It is the origin of all vocations in life. That is what Jesus was looking for in the young man when He said: "Keep the commandments" (see Mark 10:19).

In other words: Serve God and your neighbor according to all the demands of a true and upright heart. And when the young man indicated that he was already following that path, Jesus invited him to an even greater love: Leave all and come, follow Me; leave everything that concerns only yourself and join Me in the immense task of saving the world (see verse 21). Along the path of each person's existence, the Lord has something for each one to do. [TPS 40/3, 1995, 162]

THE WEEK OF JANUARY 31, 1999

5. IMITATE JESUS' LOVE

Jesus asks us to follow Him and to imitate Him along the path of love, a love which gives itself completely to the brethren out of love for God: "This is my commandment, that you love one another as I have loved you" (Jn 15:12). The word "as" requires imitation of Jesus and of His love, of which the washing of feet is a sign: "If I, then, your Lord and Teacher, have washed your feet, you also ought to wash one another's feet. For I have given you an example, that you also should do as I have done to you" (Jn 13:14-15).

Jesus' way of acting and His words, His deeds, and His precepts constitute the moral rule of Christian life. Indeed, His actions, and in particular His Passion and death on the Cross, are the living Revelation of His love for the Father and for others. This is exactly the love that Jesus wishes to be imitated by all who follow Him. It is the "new" commandment: "A new commandment I give to you, that you love one another; even as I have loved you, that you also love one another. By this all men will know that you are my disciples, if you have love for one another" (Jn 13:34-35)....

To imitate and live out the love of Christ is not possible for man by his own strength alone. He becomes capable of this love only by virtue of a gift received. As the Lord Jesus receives the love of His Father, so He in turn freely communicates that love to His disciples: "As the Father has loved me, so have I loved you; abide in my love" (Jn 15:9). Christ's gift is His Spirit, whose first "fruit" (Gal 5:22) is charity: "God's love has been poured into our hearts through the Holy Spirit which has been given to us" (Rom 5:5).

St. Augustine asks, "Does love bring about the keeping of the commandments or does the keeping of the commandments bring about love?" And he answers, "But who can doubt that love comes first? For the one who does not love has no reason for keeping the commandments...."[1]

Love and life according to the Gospel cannot be thought of first and foremost as a kind of precept, because what they demand is beyond man's abilities. They are possible only as the result of a gift of God who heals, restores, and transforms the human heart by His grace: "For the law was given through Moses; grace and truth came through Jesus Christ" (Jn 1:17). [VS n. 20, 22-23]

MARY, MODEL OF LOVE
Jesus has commended the Church to the love of His Blessed Mother, who invites us to return to the house of the Father.

THE WEEK OF FEBRUARY 7, 1999

6. A MOTHER'S INEXHAUSTIBLE LOVE

We can say that the mystery of the Redemption took shape beneath the heart of the Virgin of Nazareth when she pronounced her "fiat" ["let it be done"]. From then on, under the special influence of the Holy Spirit, this heart, the heart of both a virgin and a mother, has always followed the work of her Son and has gone out to all those whom Christ has embraced and continues to embrace with inexhaustible love. For that reason her heart must also have the inexhaustibility of a mother.

The special characteristic of the motherly love that the Mother of God inserts in the mystery of the Redemption and the life of the Church finds expression in its exceptional closeness to man and all that happens to him. It is in this that the mystery of the Mother consists. The Church, which looks to her with altogether special love and hope, wishes to make this mystery her own in an ever-deeper manner.... The

Father's eternal love, which has been manifested in the history of mankind through the Son whom the Father gave, "that whoever believes in him should not perish but have eternal life" (Jn 3:16), comes close to each of us through this Mother. [RH n. 22]

7. MARY'S LOVING AND URGENT INVITATION

Mary Most Holy, the highly favored daughter of the Father, [appears] before the eyes of believers as the perfect model of love towards both God and neighbor. As she herself says in the Canticle of the *Magnificat*, great things were done for her by the Almighty, whose name is holy (see Luke 1:49). The Father chose her for a unique mission in the history of salvation: that of being the Mother of the long-awaited Savior.

The Virgin responded to God's call with complete openness: "Behold, I am the handmaid of the Lord" (Lk 1:38, RSV). Her motherhood, which began in Nazareth and was lived most intensely in Jerusalem at the foot of the Cross, will be felt during this year [of preparation] as a loving and urgent invitation addressed to all the children of God, so that they will return to the house of the Father when they hear her maternal voice: "Do whatever Christ tells you" (see John 2:5). [TMA n. 54]

SIN, CONVERSION, PENANCE, AND MERCY

The journey home to God the Father is a journey of conversion from sin to holiness, from brokenness to wholeness, that travels along the way of repentance.

8. ACKNOWLEDGING OUR SIN

In spite of all the witness of creation... the spirit of darkness (see Ephesians 6:12, Luke 22:53) is capable of showing God as an enemy of His own creature, and in the first place as an enemy of man, as a source of danger and threat to man. In this way Satan manages to sow in man's soul the seed of opposition to the One who from the beginning would be considered as man's enemy—and not as Father. Man is challenged to become the adversary of God!

The analysis of sin in its original dimension indicates that, through the influence of the "father of lies," throughout the history of humanity there will be a constant pressure on man to reject God, even to the point of hating him: "Love of self to the point of contempt for God," as St. Augustine puts it.[2] Man will be inclined to see in God primarily a limitation of himself, and not the source of his own freedom and the fullness of good. [DV n. 38]

In the words of St. John the apostle, "If we say we have no sin, we deceive ourselves, and the truth is not in us. If we confess our sins, he is faithful and just, and will forgive our sins" (1 Jn 1:8-9, RSV). Written at the very dawn of the Church, these inspired words introduce better than any other human expression the theme of sin....

These words present the question of sin in its human dimension: sin as an integral part of the truth about man. But they immediately relate the human dimension to its divine dimension, where sin is countered by the truth of divine love, which is just, generous, and faithful, and which reveals itself above all in forgiveness and redemption. Thus St. John also writes a little further on that "whatever accusations [our conscience] may raise against us, God is greater than our conscience" (see 1 John 3:20).

To acknowledge one's sin, indeed… to recognize oneself as being a sinner, capable of sin and inclined to commit sin, is the essential first step in returning to God. For example, this is the experience of David, who "having done what is evil in the eyes of the Lord" and having been rebuked by the prophet Nathan (see 2 Samuel 11-12), exclaims: "For I know my transgressions, and my sin is ever before me. Against you, you alone, have I sinned and done what is evil in your sight" (see Psalms 51:5-6). Similarly, Jesus Himself puts the following significant words on the lips and in the heart of the prodigal son: "Father, I have sinned against heaven and before you" (Lk 15:18, 21).

In effect, to become reconciled with God presupposes and includes detaching oneself consciously and with determination from the sin into which one has fallen. It presupposes and includes, therefore, doing penance in the fullest sense of the term: repenting, showing this repentance, adopting a real attitude of repentance—which is the attitude of the person who starts out on the road of return to the Father. This is a general law and one which each individual must follow in his or her particular situation. For it is not possible to deal with sin and conversion only in abstract terms. [RP n. 13]

9. SIN, A WOUNDING OF THE CHURCH

Sin is... a wound inflicted upon the Church. In fact, every sin harms the holiness of the ecclesial community. Since all the faithful are in solidarity in the Christian community, there can never be a sin which does not have an effect on the whole community. If it is true that the good done by one person is a benefit and help to all the others, unfortunately it is equally true that the evil committed by one obstructs the perfection to which all are tending....

Reconciliation with God is also reconciliation with the Church, and in a certain sense with all of creation, whose harmony is violated by sin. The Church is the mediatrix of this reconciliation. It is a role assigned to her by her Founder, who gave her the mission and power of forgiving sins. Every instance of reconciliation with God thus takes place in an explicit or implicit, conscious or unconscious, relationship with the Church. [TPS 37/5, 1992, 305]

10. A PROPER SENSE OF SIN

The forgiveness of sins first experienced in baptism is a recurring need in the life of every Christian. Restoring a proper sense of sin is the first step to be taken in facing squarely the grave spiritual crisis looming over men and women today, a crisis which can well be described as "an eclipse of conscience."[3] Without a healthy awareness of their own sinfulness, people will never experience the depth of God's redeeming love for them while they were still sinners (see Romans 5:8). Given the prevailing idea that happiness consists in satisfying oneself and being satisfied with oneself, the Church must proclaim even more vigorously that it is only God's grace, not therapeutic or self-convincing schemes, which can heal the divisions in the human heart caused by sinfulness (see Romans 3:24; Ephesians 2:5). [TPS 38/6, 1993, 371]

11. THE TWOFOLD INJURY OF SIN

As a rupture with God, sin is an act of disobedience by a creature who rejects, at least implicitly, the very One from whom he came and who sustains him in life. It is therefore a suicidal act. Since by sinning man refuses to submit to God, his internal balance is also destroyed and it is precisely within himself that contradictions and conflicts arise.

Wounded in this way, man almost inevitably causes damage to the fabric of his relationship with others and with the created world. This is an objective law and an objective reality, verified in so many ways in the human psyche and in the spiritual life as well as in society, where it is easy to see the signs and effects of internal disorder.

The mystery of sin is composed of this twofold wound which the sinner opens in himself and in his relationship with his neighbor. Therefore one can speak of personal and social sin: from one point of view, every sin is personal; from another point of view, every sin is social insofar as and because it also has social repercussions....

Sin, in the proper sense, is always a personal act, since it is an act of freedom on the part of an individual person and not properly of a group or community. This individual may be conditioned, incited, and influenced by numerous and powerful external factors. He may also be subjected to tendencies, defects, and habits linked with his personal condition. In not a few cases such external and internal factors may attenuate, to a greater or lesser degree, the person's freedom and therefore his responsibility and guilt.

But it is a truth of faith, also confirmed by our experience and reason, that the human person is free. This truth cannot be disregarded in order to place the blame for individuals' sins on external factors such as structures, systems, or other people. Above all, this would be to deny the person's dignity and freedom, which are manifested—even though in a negative and disastrous way—also in this responsibility for sin committed. Hence there is nothing so personal and untransferable in each individual as merit for virtue or responsibility for sin. [RP n. 15, 16]

12. THE HUMAN CONSCIENCE

Like all things human, even [the] conscience can fail and encounter illusions and errors. It is a delicate voice that can be overpowered by a noisy, distracted way of life, or almost suffocated by a long-lasting and serious habit of sin.

Conscience needs to be nurtured and educated, and the preferred way to form it—at least for those who have the grace of faith—is to relate it to the biblical revelation of the moral law, authoritatively interpreted, with the help of the Holy Spirit, by the Magisterium of the Church. [TPS 39/3, 1993, 166]

The guarantee that objective truth exists is found in God, who is absolute Truth; objectively speaking, the search for truth and the search for God are one and the same.... Every individual has the grave duty to form his or her own conscience in the light of that objective truth which everyone can come to know, and which no one may be prevented from knowing. To claim that one has a right to act according to conscience—but without at the same time acknowledging the duty to conform one's conscience to the truth and to the law which God Himself has written on our hearts—in the end means nothing more than imposing one's limited personal opinion....

On the contrary, the truth must be passionately pursued and lived to the best of one's ability.... Freedom of conscience, rightly understood, is by its very nature always ordered to the truth....

Faced with the obligation of following their own consciences in the search for the truth, the disciples of Jesus Christ know that they may not trust only in their personal capacity for moral discernment. Revelation enlightens their consciences and enables them to know that freedom which is God's great gift to mankind. Not only has He inscribed the natural law within the heart of each individual, in that "most secret core and sanctuary of a man [where] he is alone with God,"[4] but He has also revealed His own law in the Scriptures. Here we find the call, or rather the command, to love God and to observe His law....

More than anyone else, the Christian ought to feel the obligation to conform his conscience to the truth. Before the splendor of the free gift of God's revelation in Christ, how humbly and attentively must he listen to the voice of conscience! How modest must he be in regard to his own limited insight! How quick must he be to learn and how slow to condemn! One of the constant temptations in every age, even among Christians, is to make oneself the norm of truth. In an age of pervasive individualism, this temptation takes a variety of forms. But the mark of those who are in the truth is the ability to love humbly. This is what God's Word teaches us: Truth is expressed in love (see Ephesians 4:15). [TPS 36/4, 1991, 209-210, 212, 215]

13. ARE WE REPENTANT OR SELF-SATISFIED?

We should take to heart the message of the Gospel parable of the Pharisee and the tax collector (see Luke 18:9-14). The tax collector might possibly have had some justification for the sins he committed, such as to diminish his responsibility. [Yet] his prayer does not dwell on such justifications, but rather on his own unworthiness before God's infinite holiness: "God, be merciful to me a sinner!" (Lk 18:13). The Pharisee, on the other hand, is self-justified, finding some excuse for each of his failings.

Here we encounter two different attitudes of the moral conscience of man in every age. The tax collector represents a repentant conscience, fully aware of the frailty of its own nature and seeing in its own failings, whatever their subjective justifications, a confirmation of its need for redemption. The Pharisee represents a self-satisfied conscience, under the illusion that it is able to observe the law without the help of grace and convinced that it does not need mercy.

All people must take great care not to allow themselves to be tainted by the attitude of the Pharisee, which would seek to eliminate awareness of one's own limits and of one's own sin. In our own day this attitude is expressed particularly in the attempt to adapt the moral norm to one's own capacities and personal interests, and even in the rejection of the very idea of a norm. [VS n. 104-105]

14. MARY, THE MODEL OF THE MORAL LIFE

Mary is the radiant sign and inviting model of the moral life.... Mary shares our human condition, but in complete openness to the grace of God. Not having known sin, she is able to have compassion on every kind of weakness. She understands sinful man and loves him with a mother's love.

Precisely for this reason she is on the side of truth and shares the Church's burden in recalling always and to everyone the demands of morality. Nor does she permit sinful man to be deceived by those who claim to love Him by justifying his sin, for she knows that the sacrifice of Christ her Son would thus be emptied of its power. No absolution offered by beguiling doctrines... can make man truly happy. Only the Cross and the glory of the risen Christ can grant peace to his conscience and salvation to his life. [VS n. 120]

15. CONVERSION AND PENANCE

In this third year [of preparation] the sense of being on a journey to the Father should encourage everyone to undertake, by holding fast to Christ the

Redeemer of man, a journey of authentic conversion. This includes both a negative aspect, that of liberation from sin, and a positive aspect, that of choosing good, accepting the ethical values expressed in the natural law, which is confirmed and deepened by the Gospel.

This is the proper context for a renewed appreciation and more intense celebration of the Sacrament of Penance in its most profound meaning. The call to conversion as the indispensable condition of Christian love is particularly important in contemporary society, where the very foundations of an ethically correct vision of human existence often seem to have been lost. [TMA n. 50]

Contemporary man seems to find it harder than ever to recognize his own mistakes and to decide to retrace his steps and begin again after changing course. He seems very reluctant to say "I repent" or "I am sorry." He seems to refuse instinctively and often irresistibly anything that is penance in the sense of a sacrifice accepted and carried out for the correction of sin.

In this regard I would like to emphasize that the Church's penitential discipline, even though it has been mitigated for some time, cannot be abandoned without grave harm both to the interior life of individual Christians and of the ecclesial community and also to their capacity for missionary influence. It is not uncommon for non-Christians to be surprised at the negligible witness of true penance on the part of Christ's followers. It is clear, however, that Christian penance will only be authentic if it is inspired by love and not by mere fear; if it consists in a serious effort to crucify the "old man" so that the "new" can be born by the power of Christ; if it takes as its model Christ, who though He was innocent chose the path of poverty, patience, austerity, and, one can say, the penitential life. [RP n. 26]

Recourse to the Sacrament [of Penance] is necessary when even only one mortal sin has been committed. However, the Christian who believes in the effectiveness of sacramental forgiveness has recourse to the Sacrament with a certain frequency, even when it is not a case of necessity. In it he finds the path for an increasing sensitivity of conscience and an ever-deeper purification, a source of peace, a help in resisting temptation and in striving for a life that responds more and more to the demands of the law and love of God. [TPS 37/5, 1992, p. 306]

16. THE INDIVIDUAL ASPECT OF PENANCE

In the last years much has been done to highlight in the Church's practice—in conformity with the most ancient tradition of the Church—the community aspect of penance and especially of the Sacrament of Penance. We cannot, however, forget that conversion is a particularly profound inward act in which the individual cannot be replaced by others and cannot make the community be a substitute for him. Although the participation by the fraternal community of the faithful in the penitential celebration is a great help for the act of personal conversion, nevertheless, in the final analysis, it is necessary that in this act there should be a pronouncement by the individual himself with the whole depth of his conscience and with the whole of his sense of guilt and of trust in God, placing himself like the psalmist before God to confess: "Against you... have I sinned" (see Psalms 51:6).

In faithfully observing the centuries-old practice of the Sacrament of Penance—the practice of individual confession with a personal act of sorrow and the intention to amend and make satisfaction—the Church is therefore defending the human soul's individual right. [It is] man's right to a more personal encounter with the crucified forgiving Christ, with Christ saying, through the minister of the Sacrament of Reconciliation: "Your sins are forgiven" (see Mark 2:5); "Go, and do not sin again" (see John 8:11).

As is evident, this is also a right on Christ's part with regard to every human being redeemed by Him. [It is] His right to meet each one of us in that key moment in the soul's life constituted by the moment of conversion and forgiveness. By guarding the Sacrament of Penance, the Church expressly affirms her faith in the mystery of the Redemption as a living and life-giving reality that fits in with man's inward truth, with human guilt and also with the desires of the human conscience.

"Blessed are those who hunger and thirst for righteousness, for they shall be satisfied" (see Matthew 5:6). The Sacrament of Penance is the means to satisfy man with the righteousness that comes from the Redeemer Himself. [RH n. 20]

THE WEEK OF APRIL 25, 1999

17. PENANCE, CHANNEL OF REDEMPTIVE POWER

For a Christian the Sacrament of Penance is the ordinary way of obtaining forgiveness and the remission of serious sin committed after Baptism. Certainly the

Savior and His [saving] action are not so bound to a sacramental sign as to be unable in any period or area of the history of salvation to work outside and above the sacraments. But in the school of faith we learn that the same Savior desired and provided that the simple and precious sacraments of faith would ordinarily be the effective means through which His redemptive power passes and operates.

It would therefore be foolish, as well as presumptuous, to wish arbitrarily to disregard the means of grace and salvation which the Lord has provided and, in the specific case, to claim to receive forgiveness while doing without the Sacrament which was instituted by Christ precisely for forgiveness. The renewal of the rites carried out after the [Second Vatican] Council does not sanction any illusion or alteration in this direction. According to the Church's intention, it was and is meant to stir up in each one of us a new impulse toward the renewal of our interior attitude; toward a deeper understanding of the nature of the Sacrament of Penance; toward a reception of the Sacrament which is more filled with faith, not anxious but trusting; toward a more frequent celebration of the Sacrament which is seen to be completely filled with the Lord's merciful love.... [For] every confessional is a special and blessed place from which, with divisions wiped away, there is born new and uncontaminated a reconciled individual—a reconciled world! [RP n. 31]

18. THE TRIUMPH OF MERCY

Jesus Christ was sent by the Father as the revelation of God's mercy (see John 3:16-18). Christ came not to condemn but to forgive, to show mercy (see Matthew 9:13). And the greatest mercy of all is found in His being in our midst and calling us to meet Him and to confess with Peter that He is "the Son of the living God" (Mt 16:16).

No human sin can erase the mercy of God, or prevent Him from unleashing all His triumphant power, if we only call upon Him. Indeed, sin itself makes even more radiant the love of the Father who, in order to ransom a slave, sacrificed His Son: His mercy toward us is redemption. This mercy reaches its fullness in the gift of the Spirit who bestows new life and demands that it be lived.

No matter how many and great the obstacles put in His way by human frailty and sin, the Spirit, who renews the face of the earth (see Psalms 104:30), makes possible the miracle of the perfect accomplishment of the good. This renewal, which gives the ability to do what is good, noble, beautiful, pleasing to God, and in conformity with His will, is in some way the flowering of the gift of mercy, which offers liberation from the slavery of evil and gives the strength to sin no more. Through the gift of new life, Jesus makes us sharers in His love and leads us to the Father in the Spirit. [VS n. 118]

CHRISTIAN MORAL RESPONSIBILITY

Once we have begun to deal with the roots and results of our personal sin, we are better able to identify our moral respon-sibilities in the wider world.

19. THE CHURCH MUST ACKNOWLEDGE PAST SINS

It is appropriate that, as the second millennium of Christianity draws to a close, the Church should become more fully conscious of the sinfulness of her children, recalling all those times in history when they departed from the spirit of Christ and His Gospel and, instead of offering to the world the witness of a life inspired by the values of faith, indulged in ways of thinking and acting that were truly forms of counterwitness and scandal.

Although she is holy because of her incorporation into Christ, the Church does not tire of doing penance: before God and man she always acknowledges as her own her sinful sons and daughters....

The Holy Door of the Jubilee of the Year 2000 should be symbolically wider than those of previous Jubilees, because humanity, upon reaching this goal, will leave behind not just a century but a millennium. It is fitting that the Church should make this passage with a clear awareness of what has happened to her during the last ten centuries. She cannot cross the threshold of the new millennium without encouraging her children to purify themselves, through repentance, of past errors and instances of infidelity, inconsistency, and slowness to act. Acknowledging the weaknesses of the past is an act of honesty and courage which helps us to strengthen our faith, which alerts us to face today's temptations and challenges, and prepares us to meet them....

On the threshold of the new millennium

58

Christians need to place themselves humbly before the Lord and examine themselves on the responsibility which they too have for the evils of our day. The present age, in fact, together with much light, also presents not a few shadows.

How can we remain silent, for example, about the religious indifference which causes many people today to live as if God did not exist, or to be content with a vague religiosity, incapable of coming to grips with the question of truth and the requirement of consistency? To this must be added the widespread loss of the transcendent sense of human life, and confusion in the ethical sphere, even about the fundamental values of respect for life and the family.

The sons and daughters of the Church too need to examine themselves in this regard. To what extent have they been shaped by the climate of secularism and ethical relativism? And what responsibility do they bear, in view of the increasing lack of religion, for not having shown the true face of God, by having "failed in their religious, moral, or social life"?[5]

It cannot be denied that, for many Christians, the spiritual life is passing through a time of uncertainty which affects not only their moral life but also their life of prayer and the theological correctness of their faith. Faith, already put to the test by the challenges of our times, is sometimes disoriented by erroneous theological views, the spread of which is abetted by the crisis of obedience [to] the Church's Magisterium.

And with respect to the Church of our time, how can we not lament the lack of discernment, which at times becomes even acquiescence, shown by many

Christians concerning the violation of fundamental human rights by totalitarian regimes? And should we not also regret, among the shadows of our own day, the responsibility shared by so many Christians for grave forms of injustice and exclusion? It must be asked how many Christians really know and put into practice the principles of the Church's social doctrine. [TMA n. 33, 36]

20. CLEAR MORAL TEACHING IS LIBERATING

One of the key pastoral problems facing us is the widespread misunderstanding of the role of conscience, whereby individual conscience and experience are exalted above or against Church teaching. The young men and women of America, and indeed of the whole Western world, who are often victims of educational theories which propose that they "create" their own values and that feeling good about themselves is a primary guiding moral principle, are asking to be led out of this moral confusion.

All those who teach in the name of the Church should fearlessly honor the dignity of the moral conscience as the sanctuary in which the voice of God is heard. But with equal care they should proclaim, in opposition to all subjectivism, that conscience is not a tribunal which creates the good, but must be formed in the light of universal and objective norms of morality. Clear teaching on these matters is also an essential part of the necessary return to the practice of the Sacrament of Penance....

Clear teaching on all such matters is liberating because it presents the true meaning of discipleship: Christ calls His followers to friendship with Him (see

John 15:15). In fact, the personal following of Christ is the essential foundation of Christian morality. The "obedience of faith" (Rom 16:26) is both an intellectual assent to doctrine as well as a life commitment which draws us into evermore perfect union with Christ Himself. The Church must always be careful not to reduce "the word of truth" (see Colossians 1:5) to an abstract code of ethics and morality, or a treatise of rules for good behavior. The preaching of Christian morality, so closely linked to the new evangelization, must not empty the Cross of Christ of its power (see 1 Corinthians 1:17). [TPS 39/2, 1994, 117]

At times, in the discussions about new and complex moral problems, it can seem that Christian morality is in itself too demanding, difficult to understand, and almost impossible to practice. This is untrue, since Christian morality consists, in the simplicity of the Gospel in following Jesus Christ, in abandoning oneself to Him, in letting oneself be transformed by His grace and renewed by His mercy—gifts which come to us in the living communion of His Church.... By the light of the Holy Spirit, the living essence of Christian morality can be understood by everyone, even the least learned, but particularly those who are able to preserve an "undivided heart" (see Psalms 86:11). [VS n. 119]

THE FAMILY

If we are to bring healing to a world so deeply loved by the Father, we cannot neglect to care for the family, the foundation of society.

21. MARRIAGE, SIGN OF CHRIST'S LOVE FOR THE CHURCH

Christ's love is the source and the foundation of the love uniting... spouses. It should be stressed that true conjugal love is meant [here], and not mere spontaneous impulse. Today sexuality is often exalted to the point of obscuring the profound nature of love. Certainly, sexual life too has its own genuine value, which can never be underestimated, but it is a limited value that is an insufficient basis for the marriage union, which by its nature depends on total personal commitment.

Every sound psychology and philosophy of love is in agreement on this point. Christian teaching also emphasizes the qualities of the individuals' unitive love and casts a higher light on it, raising it—by virtue of a sacrament—to the level of grace and of sharing in the divine love of Christ. Along these lines St. Paul says of marriage: "This is a great mystery" (Ephesians 5:32), in reference to Christ and the Church. For the Christian, this theological mystery is at the root of the ethics of marriage, conjugal love, and sexual life itself: "Husbands, love your wives, as Christ loved the Church and gave himself up for her" (Eph 5:25).

Grace and the sacramental bond enable conjugal life, as a sign of and share in the love of Christ the Bridegroom, to be a way of holiness for Christian spouses and at the same time to be an effective incentive for the Church to invigorate the communion of the love that distinguishes her. [TPS 40/1, 1995, 27-28]

22. AN INDISSOLUBLE COMMUNION

It is a fundamental duty of the Church to reaffirm strongly... the doctrine of the indissolubility of marriage. To all those who in our times consider it too difficult or indeed impossible to be bound to one person for the whole of life, and to those caught up in a culture that rejects the indissolubility of marriage and openly mocks the commitment of spouses to fidelity, it is necessary to reconfirm the good news of the definitive nature of that conjugal love that has in Christ its foundation and strength.

Being rooted in the personal and total self-giving of the couple and being required by the good of the children, the indissolubility of marriage finds its ultimate truth in the plan that God has manifested in His Revelation: He wills and He communicates the indissolubility of marriage as a fruit, a sign, and a requirement of the absolutely faithful love that God has for man and that the Lord Jesus has for the Church....

The gift of the Sacrament [of Matrimony] is at the same time a vocation and commandment for the Christian spouses, that they may remain faithful to each other forever, beyond every trial and difficulty, in generous obedience to the holy will of the Lord: "What therefore God has joined together, let not man put asunder" (Mt 19:6).

To bear witness to the inestimable value of the indissolubility and fidelity of marriage is one of the most precious and most urgent tasks of Christian couples in our time.... I praise and encourage those numerous couples who, though encountering no small difficulty, preserve and develop the value of indissolubility. Thus in a humble and courageous manner they perform the role committed to them of being a sign—a small and precious sign, sometimes also subjected to temptation, but always renewed—of the unfailing fidelity with which God and Jesus Christ love each and every human being.

But it is also proper to recognize the value of the witness of those spouses who, even when abandoned by their partner, with the strength of faith and of Christian hope have not entered a new union: These spouses too give an authentic witness to fidelity, of which the world today has a great need. For this reason they must be encouraged and helped by the pastors and the faithful of the Church. [FC n. 20]

23. THE TRIALS OF MARRIAGE CAN BE REDEMPTIVE

We must remember that, since the love of Christ the Bridegroom for the Church is a redemptive love, the love of Christian spouses becomes an active participation in Redemption.

Redemption is tied to the Cross: and this helps us to understand and appreciate the meaning of the trials that the couple's life is certainly not spared, but which in God's plan are meant to reinforce their love and bring greater fruitfulness to their married life. Far from promising his married followers an earthly paradise, Jesus Christ offers them the opportunity and the vocation to make a journey with Him which, through difficulties and suffering, will strengthen their union and lead them to a greater joy, as proven by the experience of so many Christian couples, in our day as well. [TPS 40/1, 1995, 28-29]

24. MARRIAGE AND VIRGINITY OR CELIBACY

Virginity or celibacy for the sake of the Kingdom of God not only does not contradict the dignity of marriage but presupposes it and confirms it. Marriage and virginity or celibacy are two ways of expressing and living the one mystery of the covenant of God with His people. When marriage is not esteemed, neither can consecrated virginity or celibacy exist; when human sexuality is not regarded as a great value given by the Creator, the renunciation of it for the sake of the Kingdom of heaven loses its meaning....

Christian couples.... have the right to expect from celibate persons a good example and a witness of fidelity to their vocation until death. Just as fidelity at times becomes difficult for married people and requires sacrifice, mortification, and self-denial, the same can happen to celibate persons, and their fidelity, even in the trials that may occur, should strengthen the fidelity of married couples.

These reflections on virginity or celibacy can enlighten and help those who, for reasons independent of their own will, have been unable to marry and have then accepted their situation in a spirit of service. [FC n. 16]

25. THE SOVEREIGNTY OF THE FAMILY

A person normally comes into the world within a family, and can be said to owe to the family the very fact of his existing as an individual. When he has no family, the person coming into the world develops an

anguished sense of pain and loss, one which will subsequently burden his whole life.

The Church draws near with loving concern to all
who experience situations such as these, for she
knows well the fundamental role which the family is
called upon to play. Furthermore, she knows that a
person goes forth from the family in order to realize
in a new family unit his particular vocation in life.
Even if someone chooses to remain single, the family
continues to be, as it were, his existential horizon,
that fundamental community in which the whole
network of social relations is grounded, from the
closest and most immediate to the most distant....

Every effort should be made so that the family will
be recognized as the primordial and, in a certain
sense, sovereign society. The sovereignty of the family is essential for the good of society. A truly sovereign and spiritually vigorous nation is always made
up of strong families who are aware of their vocation
and mission in history. [TPS 39/4, 1994, 208, 232]

THE WEEK OF JUNE 27, 1999

26. SPIRITUAL FORMATION IN THE FAMILY

The Christian family, as the "domestic Church,..."
makes up a natural and fundamental school for formation in the faith. Father and mother receive from
the Sacrament of Matrimony the grace and the ministry of the Christian education of their children
before whom they bear witness and to whom they
transmit both human and religious values. While
learning their first words, children learn also the
praise of God, whom they feel is near them as a loving and providential Father. While learning the first

acts of love, children also learn to open themselves to others, and through the gift of self receive the sense of living as a human being.

The daily life itself of a truly Christian family makes up the first experience of Church, intended to find confirmation and development in an active and responsible process of the children's introduction into the wider ecclesial community and civil society. The more that Christian spouses and parents grow in the awareness that their "domestic Church" participates in the life and mission of the universal Church, so much the more will their sons and daughters be able to be formed in a sense of the Church and will perceive all the beauty of dedicating their energies to the service of the Kingdom of God. [CL n. 62]

The family's catechetical activity has a special character, which is in a sense irreplaceable.... Education in the faith by parents, which should begin from the children's tenderest age, is already being given when the members of a family help each other to grow in faith through the witness of their Christian lives, a witness that is often without words but which perseveres throughout a day-to-day life lived in accordance with the Gospel. This catechesis is more incisive when, in the course of family events (such as the reception of the sacraments, the celebration of the great liturgical feasts, the birth of a child, a bereavement) care is taken to explain in the home the Christian or religious content of these events.

But that is not enough: Christian parents must strive to follow and repeat, within the setting of family life, the more methodical teaching received elsewhere. The fact that these truths about the main questions of faith and Christian living are thus repeated within a family setting impregnated with love and respect will often make it possible to influence the children in a decisive way for life. The parents themselves profit from the effort that this demands of them, for in a catechetical dialogue of this sort each individual both receives and gives.

Family catechesis therefore precedes, accompanies, and enriches all other forms of catechesis. Furthermore, in places where antireligious legislation endeavors even to prevent education in the faith, and in places where widespread unbelief or invasive secularism makes real religious growth practically impossible, "the church of the home"[6] remains the one place where children and young people can receive an authentic catechesis. Thus there cannot be too great an effort on the part of Christian parents to prepare for this ministry of being their own children's catechists and to carry it out with tireless zeal. [CT n. 68]

THE WEEK OF JULY 4, 1999

27. FAMILY PRAYER

Family prayer has its own characteristic qualities. It is prayer offered in common, husband and wife together, parents and children together. Communion in prayer is both a consequence of and a requirement for the communion bestowed by the Sacraments of Baptism and Matrimony. The words with which the Lord Jesus promises His presence can be applied to the members of the Christian family in a special way: "Again I say to you, if two of you agree on earth about anything they ask, it will be done for them by my Father in heaven. For where two or three are gathered in my name, there am I in the midst of them" (Mt 18:19-20].

Family prayer has for its very own object family life itself, which in all its varying circumstances is seen as a call from God and lived as a filial response to His call. Joys and sorrows, hopes and disappointments, births and birthday celebrations, wedding anniversaries of the parents, departures, separations and homecomings, important and far-reaching decisions, the death of those who are dear... all of these mark God's loving intervention in the family's history. They should be seen as suitable moments for thanksgiving, for petition, for trusting abandonment of the family into the hands of their common Father in heaven. The dignity and responsibility of the Christian family as the domestic Church can be achieved only with God's unceasing aid, which will surely be granted if it is humbly and trustingly petitioned in prayer....

By reason of their dignity and mission, Christian parents have the specific responsibility of educating their children in prayer, introducing them to gradual discovery of the mystery of God and to personal dialogue with Him.... The concrete example and living witness of parents is fundamental and irreplaceable in educating their children to pray. Only by praying together with their children can a father and mother—exercising their royal priesthood—penetrate the innermost depths of their children's hearts and leave an impression that the future events in their lives will not be able to efface. [FC n. 59, 60]

28. HONOR WITHIN THE FAMILY

The family is a community of particularly intense interpersonal relationships: between spouses, between parents and children, between generations. It is a community which must be safeguarded in a special way. And God cannot find a better safeguard than this: Honor.

"Honor your father and your mother, that your days may be long in the land which the Lord your God gives to you" (Ex 20:12).... The fourth commandment is closely linked to the commandment of love.... Honor is essentially an attitude of unselfishness. It could be said that it is a sincere gift of person to person, and in that sense honor converges with love.... You parents, the divine precept seems to say, should act in such a way that your life will merit the honor (and the love) of your children! Do not let the divine command that you be honored fall into a moral vacuum! Ultimately then we are speaking of mutual honor.

The commandment "Honor your father and your mother" indirectly tells parents: Honor your sons and your daughters. They deserve this because they are alive, because they are who they are, and this is true from the first moment of their conception. The fourth commandment, then, by expressing the intimate bonds uniting the family, highlights the basis of its inner unity. [TPS 39/4, 1994, 225-6]

29. THE ROLES OF FATHER AND MOTHER

Within the... family... the man is called upon to live his gift and role as husband and father. In his wife he sees the fulfillment of God's intention: "It is not good that the man should be alone; I will make him a helper fit for him" (Gn 2:18), and he makes his own the cry of Adam, the first husband: "This at last is bone of my bones and flesh of my flesh" (Gn 2:23)....

Love for his wife as mother of their children and love for the children themselves are for the man the natural way of understanding and fulfilling his own fatherhood. Above all where social and cultural conditions so easily encourage a father to be less concerned with his family or at any rate less involved in the work of education, efforts must be made to restore socially the conviction that the place and task of the father in and for the family is of unique and irreplaceable importance.

As experience teaches, the absence of a father causes psychological and moral imbalance and notable difficulties in family relationships. [So also] does, in contrary circumstances, the oppressive presence of a father, especially where there still prevails the phenomenon of "machismo," or a wrong superiority of male prerogatives which humiliates women and inhibits the development of healthy family relationships.

In revealing and in reliving on earth the very fatherhood of God, a man is called upon to ensure the harmonious and united development of all the members of the family: He will perform this task by exercising generous responsibility for the life conceived under the heart of the mother; by a more solicitous commitment to education, a task he shares with his wife; by work which is never a cause of division in the family but promotes its unity and stability; and by means of the witness he gives of an adult Christian life which effectively introduces the children into the living experience of Christ and the Church. [FC n. 25]

In rearing children, mothers have a singularly important role. Through the special relationship uniting a mother and her child, particularly in its earliest years of life, she gives the child that sense of security and trust without which the child would find it difficult to develop properly its own personal identity and, subsequently, to establish positive and fruitful relationships with others. This primary relationship between mother and child also has a very particular educational significance in the religious sphere, for it can direct the mind and heart of the child to God long before any formal religious education begins.

In this decisive and sensitive task, no mother should be left alone. Children need the presence and care of both parents, who carry out their duty as educators above all through the influence of the way they live. The quality of the relationship between the spouses has profound psychological effects on children and greatly conditions both the way they relate to their surroundings and the other relationships which they will develop throughout life. [TPS 40/3, 1995, 136-7]

30. THE WORK OF MOTHERS
Experience confirms that there must be a social reevaluation of the mother's role, of the toil connect-

ed with it, and of the need that children have for care, love, and affection in order that they may develop into responsible, morally and religiously mature, and psychologically stable persons. It will redound to the credit of society to make it possible for a mother—without inhibiting her freedom, without psychological or practical discrimination, and without penalizing her as compared with other women—to devote herself to taking care of her children and educating them in accordance with their needs, which vary with age. Having to abandon these tasks in order to take up paid work outside the home is wrong from the point of view of the good of society and of the family when it contradicts or hinders these primary goals of the mission of a mother....

The true advancement of women requires that labor should be structured in such a way that women do not have to pay for their advancement by abandoning what is specific to them and at the expense of the family, in which women as mothers have an irreplaceable role. [LE n. 19]

31. THE ROLE OF CHILDREN

According to the plan of God, marriage is the foundation of the wider community of the family, since the very institution of marriage and conjugal love is ordained to the procreation and education of children, in whom it finds its crowning.

In its most profound reality, love is essentially a gift; and conjugal love, while leading the spouses to the reciprocal "knowledge" which makes them "one flesh" (Gn 2:24), does not end with the couple, because it makes them capable of the greatest possible gift, the gift by which they become cooperators with God for giving life to a new human person. Thus the couple, while giving themselves to one another, give not just themselves but also the reality of children, who are a living reflection of their love, a permanent sign of conjugal unity and a living and inseparable synthesis of their being a father and a mother.

When they become parents, spouses receive from God the gift of a new responsibility. Their parental love is called to become for the children the visible sign of the very love of God, "from whom every family in heaven and on earth is named" (Eph 3:15). [FC n. 14]

Children are certainly the object of the Lord Jesus' tender and generous love. To them He gave His blessing, and even more, to them He promised the Kingdom of heaven (see Matthew 19:13-15; Mark 10:14). In particular, Jesus exalted the active role that little ones have in the Kingdom of God.

They are the eloquent symbol and exalted image of those moral and spiritual conditions that are essential for entering into the Kingdom of God and for living the logic of total confidence in the Lord: "Truly, I say to you, unless you turn and become like children, you will never enter the kingdom of heaven. Whoever humbles himself like this child, he is the greatest in the kingdom of heaven" (Mt 18:3-5; see also Luke 9:48).

Children are a continual reminder that the missionary fruitfulness of the Church has its life-giving basis not in human means and merits, but in the

absolute gratuitous gift of God. The life itself of inno-
cence and grace of many children, and even the suffering and oppression unjustly inflicted upon them,
are in virtue of the Cross of Christ a source of spiritual enrichment for them and for the entire Church.
[CL n. 47]

32. YOUTH NEED A HIGH MORAL VISION
The well-being of the world's children and young
people must be of immense concern to all who have
public responsibilities. In my pastoral visits to the
Church in every part of the world I have been deeply
moved by the almost universal conditions of difficulty in which young people grow up and live. Too
many sufferings are visited upon them by natural
calamities, famines, epidemics, by economic and
political crises, by the atrocities of war....

Where material conditions are at least adequate,
other obstacles arise, not the least of which is the
breakdown of family values and stability. In developed countries, a serious moral crisis is already
affecting the lives of many young people, leaving
them adrift, often without hope, and conditioned to
look only for immediate gratification.

Yet everywhere there are young men and women
deeply concerned about the world around them,
ready to give the best of themselves in service to others and particularly sensitive to life's transcendent
meaning. But how do we help them? Only by instill-
ing a high moral vision can a society ensure that its
young people are given the possibility to mature as
free and intelligent human beings, endowed with a

robust sense of responsibility to the common good, capable of working with others to create a community and a nation with a strong moral fiber.

America was built on such a vision, and the American people possess the intelligence and will to meet the challenge of rededicating themselves with renewed vigor to fostering the truths on which this country was founded and by which it grew. Those truths are enshrined in the Declaration of Independence, the Constitution, and the Bill of Rights, and they still today receive a broad consensus among Americans. Those truths sustain values which have led people all over the world to look to America with hope and respect.

To all Americans, without exception, I present this invitation: Let us pause and reason together (see Isaiah 1:18). To educate without a value system based on truth is to abandon young people to moral confusion, personal insecurity, and easy manipulation. No country, not even the most powerful, can endure if it deprives its own children of this essential good. Respect for the dignity and worth of every person, integrity and responsibility, as well as understanding, compassion, and solidarity toward others, survive only if they are passed on in families, in schools, and through the communications media. [PS 39/2, 1994, 85-86]

THE WEEK OF AUGUST 15, 1999
33. THE SPECIAL ROLE OF OLDER PEOPLE
Older people [are] oftentimes unjustly considered as unproductive if not directly an insupportable burden. I remind older people that the Church calls

and expects them to continue to exercise their mission in the apostolic and missionary life. This is not only a possibility for them, but it is their duty even in this time in their life when age itself provides opportunities in some specific and basic way.

The Bible delights in presenting the older person as the symbol of someone rich in wisdom and fear of the Lord (see Sirach 25:4-6). In this sense the gift of older people can be specifically that of being witness to tradition in the faith, both in the Church and in society (see Psalms 44:2; Exodus 12:26-27), the teacher of the lessons of life (see Sirach 6:34, 8:11-12), and the worker of charity.

At this moment the growing number of older people in different countries worldwide and the expected retirement of persons from various professions and the workplace provides older people with a new opportunity in the apostolate. Involved in the task is their determination to overcome the temptation of taking refuge in a nostalgia—in a never-to-return past—or fleeing from present responsibility because of difficulties encountered in a world of one novelty after another. They must always have a clear knowledge that one's role in the Church and society does not stop at a certain age at all, but at such times knows only new ways of application. As the psalmist says: "They still bring forth fruit in old age, they are ever full of sap and green, to show that the Lord is upright" (see Psalms 92:14-16).... [CL n. 48]

We should remember, as old people, that with health problems and the decline of our physical strength, we are particularly associated with Christ in His Passion and on the Cross. It is therefore possible to penetrate evermore deeply into this mystery of the redeeming sacrifice and to give the witness of faith in this mystery, of the courage and hope that derive from it in the various difficulties and trials of old age.

Everything in the life of the elderly person may serve to fulfill his earthly mission. Nothing is in vain. On the contrary, his cooperation, precisely because it is hidden, is yet more valuable for the Church. [TPS 40/1, 1995, 39]

WOMEN

As the dawn of the third millennium approaches, throughout the world the aspirations of many women once silenced are at last being heard—hopes for justice, for peace, and for an affirmation of the dignity of womanhood. In reflecting on God's love for humanity, we hear His own desire for these aspirations to be realized.

THE WEEK OF AUGUST 22, 1999

34. THE CHURCH IS GRATEFUL FOR WOMEN

The Church gives thanks for each and every woman: for mothers, for sisters, for wives; for women consecrated to God in virginity; for women dedicated to the many human beings who await the gratuitous love of another person; for women who watch over the human persons in the family, which is the fundamental sign of the human community; for women who work professionally, and who at times are burdened by a great social responsibility; for "perfect" women and for "weak" women—for all women as they have come forth from the heart of God in all the beauty and richness of their femininity; as they have been embraced by His eternal love; as, together with men, they are pilgrims on this earth, which is the temporal "homeland" of all people and is transformed sometimes into a "valley of tears"; as they assume, together with men, a common responsibility for the destiny of humanity according to daily necessities and according to that definitive destiny which the human family has in God Himself, in the bosom of the ineffable Trinity.

The Church gives thanks for all the manifestations of the feminine genius which have appeared in the course of history, in the midst of all peoples and nations. She gives thanks for all the charisms which the Holy Spirit distributes to women in the history of the People of God, for all the victories which she owes to their faith, hope, and charity. She gives thanks for all the fruits of feminine holiness.

The Church asks at the same time that these invaluable manifestations of the Spirit (see 1 Corinthians 12:4ff), which with great generosity are poured forth upon the daughters of the eternal Jerusalem, may be attentively recognized and appreciated so that they may return for the common good of the Church and of humanity, especially in our times. Meditating on the biblical mystery of the woman, the Church prays that in this mystery all women may discover themselves and their supreme vocation. [MD n. 31]

35. ADVANCING THE DIGNITY OF WOMEN

If anyone has [the] task of advancing the dignity of women in the Church and society, it is women them-

79

selves who must recognize their responsibility as leading characters. There is still much effort to be done in many parts of the world and in various surroundings to destroy that unjust and deleterious mentality which considers the human being as a thing, as an object to buy and sell, as an instrument for selfish interests or for pleasure only. Women themselves, for the most part, are the prime victims of such a mentality. Only through openly acknowledging the personal dignity of women is the first step taken to promote the full participation of women in Church life as well as in social and public life....

The awareness that women with their own gifts and tasks have their own specific vocation has increased and been deepened in the years following the [Second Vatican] Council and has found its fundamental inspiration in the Gospel and the Church's history. In fact, for the believer, the Gospel—namely, the word and example of Jesus Christ—remains the necessary and decisive point of reference. In no other moment in history is this fact more fruitful and innovative.

Though not called to the apostolate of the Twelve, and thereby to the ministerial priesthood, many women nevertheless accompanied Jesus in His ministry and assisted the group of Apostles (see Luke 8:2-3); were present at the foot of the Cross (see Luke 23:49); assisted at the burial of Christ (see Luke 23:55); received and transmitted the message of Resurrection on Easter morn (see Luke 24:1-10); and prayed with the Apostles in the Cenacle awaiting Pentecost (see Acts 1:14).

From the evidence of the Gospel, the Church at

its origin detached herself from the culture of the time and called women to tasks connected with spreading the Gospel. In his letters the Apostle Paul even cites by name a great number of women for their various functions in service of the primitive Christian community (see Romans 16:1-5; Philippians 4:2-3; Colossians 4:15; 1 Corinthians 11:5; 1 Timothy 5:16). "If the witness of the Apostles founds the Church," stated Paul VI, "the witness of women contributes greatly towards nourishing the faith of Christian communities."[7]

Both in her earliest days and in her successive development, the Church, albeit in different ways and with diverse emphases, has always known women who have exercised an oftentimes decisive role in the Church herself and accomplished tasks of considerable value on her behalf. History is marked by grand works, quite often lowly and hidden, but not for this reason any less decisive to the growth and the holiness of the Church. It is necessary that this history continue, indeed that it be expanded and intensified in the face of the growing and widespread awareness of the personal dignity of woman and her vocation, particularly in light of the urgency of a reevangelization and a major effort toward humanizing social relations. [CL n. 49]

THE WEEK OF SEPTEMBER 5, 1999

36. Special Tasks Entrusted to Women

Two great tasks entrusted to women merit the attention of everyone. First of all, the task of bringing full dignity to the conjugal life and to motherhood. Today new possibilities are opened to women for a deeper understanding and a richer realization of human and Christian values implied in the conjugal life and the experience of motherhood. Man himself—husband and father—can be helped to overcome forms of absenteeism and of periodic presence as well as a partial fulfillment of parental responsibilities—indeed, he can be involved in new and significant relations of interpersonal communion—precisely as the result of the intelligent, loving, and decisive intervention of woman.

Secondly, women have the task of assuring the moral dimension of culture, the dimension—namely of a culture worthy of the person—of an individual yet social life...."It is not good for man to be alone: let us make him a helper fit for him" (see Genesis 2:18). God entrusted the human being to woman. Certainly, every human being is entrusted to each and every other human being, but in a special way the human being is entrusted to woman, precisely because the woman in virtue of her special experience of motherhood is seen to have a specific sensitivity toward the human person and all that constitutes the individual's true welfare, beginning with the fundamental value of life. How great are the possibilities and responsibilities of woman in this area at a time when the development of science and technology is not always inspired and measured by true wisdom, with the inevitable risk of dehumanizing human life, above all when it would demand a more intense love and a more generous acceptance.

The participation of women in the life of the Church and society in the sharing of her gifts is likewise the path necessary for her personal fulfillment—on which so many justly insist today—and the basic contribution of woman to the enrichment of Church communion and dynamism in the apostolate of the People of God. [CL n. 51]

CHRISTIAN SOCIAL ACTION

To share the heart of the Father is to share His concern for those most in need—in need, not only of material goods, but of healing and reconciliation as well.

THE WEEK OF SEPTEMBER 12, 1999

37. CARING FOR THOSE MOST IN NEED

In the presence of suffering we cannot remain indifferent or passive. Before asking about the responsibility of others, believers listen to the voice of their Divine Master, who urges them to imitate the Good Samaritan, who dismounted in order to help the man who had been attacked by robbers on the road from Jerusalem to Jericho and spent his energy, time, and money for him. First and foremost he offered him his compassionate heart (see Luke 10:30-37). Christians know they are called to put Christ's teaching into practice: "Whatever you did for one of these least brothers of mine, you did for me" (see Matthew 25:40)....

Jesus came to proclaim the Gospel to the poor, to those who, aware of their limitations, feel the need of help from on high. Only the person who is poor in this sense, who is not proud or self-inflated, can understand that the wealth of light and grace received from God calls in turn for a free offering of one's life for others.

For believers this is both an individual and a social duty. The example comes from the primitive Church, which gathered around the Apostles not only to hear their preaching and celebrate the Eucharist but also to exercise charity with them. For this purpose they laid their possessions at the feet of the Apostles so that they could be distributed in turn to the poor. [TPS 38/3, 1993, 170]

The option or love of preference for the poor.... is an option, or a special form of primacy in the exercise of Christian charity, to which the whole tradition of the Church bears witness. It affects the life of each Christian inasmuch as he or she seeks to imitate the life of Christ, but it applies equally to our social responsibilities and hence to our manner of living, and to the logical decisions to be made concerning the ownership and use of goods....

It is necessary to state once more the characteristic principle of Christian social doctrine: the goods of this world are originally meant for all. The right to private property is valid and necessary, but it does not nullify the value of this principle. [SRS n. 42]

As far as the Church is concerned, the social message of the Gospel must not be considered a theory, but above all else a basis and a motivation for action. Inspired by this message, some of the first Christians distributed their goods to the poor, bearing witness to the fact that, despite different social origins, it was possible for people to live together in peace and harmony. Through the power of God, down the centuries monks tilled the land, men and women religious founded hospitals and shelters for the poor, confraternities as well as individual men and women of all states of life devoted themselves to the needy and to those on the margins of society—convinced as they were that Christ's words "As you did it to one of the least of these my brethren, you did it to me" (Mt 25:40) were not intended to remain a pious wish but were meant to become a concrete life commitment. [CA n. 57]

38. NO RECONCILIATION WITHOUT CONVERSION

Sacred Scripture speaks to us of... reconciliation, inviting us to make every effort to attain it. But Scripture also tells us that it is above all a merciful gift of God to humanity. The history of salvation— the salvation of the whole of humanity as well as of every human being of whatever period—is the wonderful history of a reconciliation: the reconciliation whereby God, as Father, in the blood and the Cross of His Son made man, reconciles the world to Himself and thus brings into being a new family of those who have been reconciled.

Reconciliation becomes necessary because there has been the break of sin from which derive all the other forms of break within man and about him. Reconciliation, therefore, in order to be complete necessarily requires liberation from sin, which is to be rejected in its deepest roots. Thus a close internal link unites conversion and reconciliation. It is impossible to split these two realities or to speak of one and say nothing of the other....

There can be no union among people without an internal change in each individual. Personal conversion is the necessary path to harmony between individuals. When the Church proclaims the good news of reconciliation or proposes achieving it through the sacraments, she is exercising a truly prophetic role: condemning the evils of man in their infected source; showing the root of divisions; and bringing hope in the possibility of overcoming tensions and conflict and reaching brotherhood, concord, and peace at all levels and in all sections of human society.

She is changing a historical condition of hatred and violence into a civilization of love. She is offering to everyone the evangelical and sacramental principle of that reconciliation at the source, from which comes every other gesture or act of reconciliation, also at the social level. [RP n. 4]

THE SPHERES OF HUMAN LIFE:
POLITICS, ECONOMICS, CULTURE, SCIENCE
To labor for the coming of God's Kingdom is to seek to penetrate every sphere of human endeavor with values that affirm the Father's love for the world.

THE WEEK OF SEPTEMBER 26, 1999
39. CHARITY AND JUSTICE IN PUBLIC LIFE
A charity that loves and serves the person is never able to be separated from justice. Each in its own way demands the full, effective acknowledgement of the rights of the individual to which society is ordered in all its structures and institutions.

In order to achieve their task directed to the Christian animation of the temporal order, in the sense of serving persons and society, the lay faithful are never to relinquish their participation in public life, that is, in the many different economic, social, legislative, administrative, and cultural areas which are intended to promote organically and institutionally the common good.... Every person has a right and duty to participate in public life, albeit in a diversity and complementarity of forms, levels, tasks, and responsibilities. Charges of careerism, idolatry of power, egoism, and corruption that are oftentimes directed at persons in government, parliaments, the ruling classes, or political parties—as well as the common opinion that participating in politics is an absolute moral danger—do not in the least justify either skepticism or an absence on the part of Christians in public life. [CL n. 42]

THE WEEK OF OCTOBER 3, 1999

40. THE CHRISTIAN IN POLITICS

The spirit of service is a fundamental element in the exercise of political power. This spirit of service, together with the necessary competence and efficiency, can make virtuous or above criticism the activity of persons in public life which is justly demanded by the rest of the people. To accomplish this requires a full-scale battle and a determination to overcome every temptation, such as the recourse to disloyalty and to falsehood; the waste of public funds for the advantage of a few and those with special interests; and the use of ambiguous and illicit means for acquiring, maintaining, and increasing power at any cost....

The lay faithful must bear witness to those human

and Gospel values that are intimately connected with political activity itself, such as liberty and justice, solidarity, faithful and unselfish dedication for the good of all, a simple lifestyle, and a preferential love for the poor and the least. This demands that the lay faithful always be more animated by a real participation in the life of the Church and enlightened by her social doctrine. In this they can be supported and helped by the nearness of the Christian community and their pastors. [CL n. 42]

When people think they possess the secret of a perfect social organization which makes evil impossible, they also think that they can use any means, including violence and deceit, in order to bring that organization into being. Politics then becomes a secular religion which operates under the illusion of creating paradise in this world. But no political society—which possesses its own autonomy and laws—can ever be confused with the Kingdom of God.

The Gospel parable of the weeds among the wheat (see Matthew 13:24-30, 36-43) teaches that it is for God alone to separate the subjects of the Kingdom from the subjects of the Evil One, and that this judgment will take place at the end of time. By presuming to anticipate judgment here and now, people put themselves in the place of God and set themselves against the patience of God.

Through Christ's sacrifice on the Cross, the victory of the Kingdom of God has been achieved once and for all. Nevertheless, the Christian life involves a struggle against temptation and the forces of evil. Only at the end of history will the Lord return in glory for the final judgment (see Matthew 25:31) with the establishment of a new heaven and a new earth (see 2 Peter 3:13; Revelation 21:1). But as long as time lasts, the struggle between good and evil continues even in the human heart itself. [CA n. 25]

Authentic democracy is possible only in a State ruled by law and on the basis of a correct conception of the human person. It requires that the necessary conditions be present for the advancement... of the individual through education and formation in true ideals, and... through the creation of structures of participation and shared responsibility.

Nowadays there is a tendency to claim that agnosticism and skeptical relativism are the philosophy and the basic attitude which correspond to democratic forms of political life. Those who are convinced that they know the truth and firmly adhere to it are considered unreliable from a democratic point of view, since they do not accept that truth is determined by the majority, or that it is subject to variation according to different political trends. [But] it must be observed in this regard that if there is no ultimate truth to guide and direct political activity, then ideas and convictions can easily be manipulated for reasons of power. As history demonstrates, a democracy without values easily turns into open or thinly disguised totalitarianism. [CA n. 46]

THE WEEK OF OCTOBER 10, 1999
41. THE CHRISTIAN IN THE WORKPLACE
In the context of the transformations taking place in the world of economy and work which are a cause of concern, the lay faithful have the responsibility of being in the forefront in working out a solution to

the very serious problems of growing unemployment; to fight for the most opportune overcoming of numerous injustices that come from organizations of work which lack a proper goal; to make the workplace become a community of persons respected in their uniqueness and in their right to participation; to develop new solidarity among those that participate in a common work; to raise up new forms of business enterprising and to look again at systems of commerce, finance, and exchange of technology. To such an end the lay faithful must accomplish their work with professional competence, with human honesty, with a Christian spirit, and especially as a way of their own sanctification.... [CL n. 43]

The Church acknowledges the legitimate role of profit as an indication that a business is functioning well. When a firm makes a profit, this means that production factors have been properly employed and corresponding human needs have been duly satisfied.

But profitability is not the only indicator of a firm's condition. It is possible for the financial accounts to be in order, and yet for the people—who make up the firm's most valuable asset—to be humiliated and their dignity offended.

Besides being morally inadmissible, this will eventually have negative repercussions on the firm's economic efficiency. In fact, the purpose of a business firm is not simply to make a profit, but is to be found in its very existence as a community of persons who in various ways are endeavoring to satisfy their basic needs, and who form a particular group at the service of the whole of society. Profit is the regulator of the life of a business, but it is not the only one. Other human and moral factors must also be considered which, in the long term, are at least equally important for the life of a business. [CA n. 35]

There are collective and qualitative needs which cannot be satisfied by market mechanisms. There are important human needs which escape its logic. There are goods which by their very nature cannot and must not be bought or sold.

Certainly the mechanisms of the market offer secure advantages: they help to utilize resources better; they promote the exchange of products; above all they give central place to the person's desires and preferences, which, in a contract, meet the desires and preferences of another person. Nevertheless, these mechanisms carry the risk of an idolatry of the market, an existence which ignores the existence of goods which by their nature are not and cannot be mere commodities. [CA n. 40]

THE WEEK OF OCTOBER 17, 1999

42. THE CHRISTIAN IN CULTURE

The Church calls upon the lay faithful to be present as signs of courage and intellectual creativity in the privileged places of culture, that is, the world of education—school and university—in places of scientific and technological research, the areas of artistic creativity and work in the humanities. Such a presence is destined not only for the recognition and possible purification of the elements that critically burden existing culture, but also for the elevation of these cultures through the riches which have their source in the Gospel and the Christian faith. [CL n. 44]

Christian wisdom, which the Church teaches by divine authority, continuously inspires the faithful of Christ zealously to endeavor to relate human affairs and activities with religious values in a single living synthesis. Under the direction of these values all things are mutually connected for the glory of God and the integral development of the human person, a development that includes both corporal and spiritual well-being.

Indeed, the Church's mission of spreading the Gospel not only demands that the Good News be preached ever more widely and to ever-greater numbers of men and women, but that the very power of the Gospel should permeate thought patterns, standards of judgment, and norms of behavior. In a word, it is necessary that the whole of human culture be steeped in the Gospel.

The cultural atmosphere in which a human being lives has a great influence upon his or her way of thinking and, thus, of acting. Therefore, a division between faith and culture is more than a small impediment to evangelization, while a culture penetrated with the Christian spirit is an instrument that favors the spreading of the Good News. [SC n. 5]

THE WEEK OF OCTOBER 24, 1999

43. SCIENCE, FAITH, AND THE
    WORLD'S FUTURE

"Science and faith are both gifts of God." This terse statement not only excludes the idea that science and faith must view one another with mutual suspicion, but also shows the deepest reason calling them to establish a constructive and cordial relationship:

God, the common foundation of both; God, the ultimate reason for the logic of creation which science explores, and the source of the Revelation by which He freely gives Himself to man, calling him to faith, in order to make him a son instead of a creature, and opening to him the gates of intimacy with Him. The light of reason, which makes science possible, and the light of Revelation, which makes faith possible, emanate from a single source....

The dialogue between science and faith, each respecting the other's areas, is doubly necessary in the domain of applied science.... It is at the level of applied science that humanity experiences, for better or worse, the power of scientific knowledge. If human life is at enormous risk today, it is not because of the truth discovered through scientific research, but because of the deadly applications made of it on the technological level....

Whenever scientific activity has a positive effect on respect for and protection of human dignity, it contributes significantly to building peace. Therefore it is necessary to be tireless in promoting a scientific culture capable of looking always at the whole person and at the whole of peoples, serving the universal good and solidarity. In this regard, great importance is attached to making progress in the dialogue between science and faith.

We must work together to reestablish the connection between truth and values, between science and ethical commitment. We must all be truly convinced that progress is really such if it is at the service of the true and total well-being of individuals and of the whole human family.... Although science's main task is to seek the truth in the free and legitimate liberty belonging to it, scientists are nevertheless not permitted to prescind from the ethical implications concerning the means of their research and the use of the truths they discover. Ethical goodness is simply another name for truth sought by the practical intellect....

My well-founded hope is that the Church and the scientific community may share their wealth of knowledge and experience in an evermore intense, cordial, and fruitful dialogue so that all creatures may participate in fulfilling God's loving plan.... May... scientists who especially cultivate the intellect also cultivate love. [TPS 38/5, 1993, 296-300]

THE WEEK OF OCTOBER 31, 1999

44. RESPECT FOR CREATION

Today in an ever-increasingly acute way, the... ecological question poses itself.... Certainly humanity has received from God Himself the task of dominating the created world and cultivating the garden of the world. But this is a task that humanity must carry out in respect for the divine image received [in human nature], and therefore with intelligence and with love, assuming responsibility for the gifts that God has bestowed and continues to bestow. Humanity has in its possession a gift that must be passed on to future generations, if possible, passed on in a better condition....

The dominion granted to man by the Creator is not an absolute power, nor can one speak of a freedom to use and misuse, or to dispose of things as one pleases. The limitation imposed from the beginning by the Creator Himself and expressed symbolically by the prohibition not to "eat of the fruit of the tree" (see Genesis 2:16-17) shows clearly enough that, when it comes to the natural world, we are subject not only to biological laws but also to moral ones which cannot be violated with impunity. A true concept of development cannot ignore the use of the things of nature, the renewability of resources and the consequences of haphazard industrialization—three considerations which alert our consciences to the moral dimension of development."[8] [CL n. 43]

WITNESSES TO THE GOSPEL OF LIFE

The gospel of God's love for humanity and the gospel of life are a single and indivisible gospel.

THE WEEK OF NOVEMBER 7, 1999

45. THE WORTH OF THE HUMAN PERSON

Man is called to a fullness of life which far exceeds the dimensions of his earthly existence, because it consists in sharing the very life of God. The loftiness of this supernatural vocation reveals the greatness and the inestimable value of human life even in its temporal phase....

The Church knows that this Gospel of life, which she has received from her Lord, has a profound and persuasive echo in the heart of every person—believer and nonbeliever alike—because it marvelously fulfills all the heart's expectations while infinitely surpassing them. Even in the midst of difficulties and uncertainties, every person sincerely open to truth and goodness can, by the light of reason and the hidden action of grace, come to recognize in the natural law written in the heart (see Romans 2:14-15) the sacred value of human life from its very beginning until its end, and can affirm the right of every human being to have this primary good respected to the highest degree. Upon the recognition of this right, every human community and the political community itself are founded....

Man's life comes from God; it is His gift, His image and imprint, a sharing in His breath of life. God therefore is the sole Lord of this life: man cannot do with it as He wills. God Himself makes this clear to Noah after the Flood: "For your own lifeblood, too, I will demand an accounting... and from man in regard to his fellowman I will demand an accounting for human life" (see Genesis 9:5). The biblical text is concerned to emphasize how the sacredness of life has its foundation in God and in his creative activity: "For God made man in his own image" (Gn 9:6).

Human life and death are thus in the hands of God, in his power: "In his hand is the life of every living thing and the breath of all mankind," exclaims Job (12:10). "The Lord brings to death and brings to life; he brings down to Sheol and raises up" (see 1 Samuel 2:6). He alone can say: "It is I who bring both death and life" (see Deuteronomy 32:39). [EV n. 2, 39]

THE WEEK OF NOVEMBER 14, 1999

46. ABORTION, AN UNSPEAKABLE CRIME

Among all the crimes which can be committed against life, procured abortion has characteristics making it particularly serious and deplorable. The Second Vatican Council defines abortion, together with infanticide, as an "unspeakable crime."[9]

But today, in many people's consciences, the perception of its gravity has become progressively obscured. The acceptance of abortion in the popular mind, in behavior, and even in law itself, is a telling sign of an extremely dangerous crisis of the moral sense, which is becoming more and more incapable of distinguishing between good and evil, even when the fundamental right to life is at stake. Given such a grave situation, we need now more than ever to have the courage to look the truth in the eye and to call things by their proper name, without yielding to convenient compromises or to the temptation of self-deception.

In this regard the reproach of the prophet is extremely straightforward: "Woe to those who call evil good and good evil, who put darkness for light and light for darkness" (Is 5:20). Especially in the case of abortion there is a widespread use of ambiguous terminology, such as "interruption of pregnancy," which tends to hide abortion's true nature and to attenuate its seriousness in public opinion. Perhaps this linguistic phenomenon is itself a symptom of an uneasiness of conscience. But no word has the power to change the reality of things: procured abortion is *the deliberate and direct killing, by whatever means it is carried out, of a human being in the initial phase of his or her existence, extending from conception to birth.*

The moral gravity of procured abortion is apparent in all its truth if we recognize that we are dealing with murder. [EV n. 58]

47. DEFEND LIFE!

America, you are beautiful and blessed in so many ways.... But your best beauty and richest blessing is found in the human person: in each man, woman, and child, in every immigrant, in every native-born son and daughter.... The ultimate test of your greatness is the way you treat every human being, but especially the weakest and most defenseless ones.

The best traditions of your land presume respect for those who cannot defend themselves. If you want equal justice for all, and true freedom and lasting peace, then, America, defend life! All the great causes that are yours today will have meaning only to the extent that you guarantee the right to life and protect the human person. [TPS 39/2, 1994, 86]

INTERRELIGIOUS DIALOGUE

Interreligious dialogue cannot replace the task of evangeliza-tion, but it is part of our demonstration of the Father's love for the people of all nations.

48. PART OF THE CHURCH'S EVANGELIZING MISSION

Interreligious dialogue is a part of the Church's evangelizing mission. Understood as a method and means of mutual knowledge and enrichment, dialogue is not in opposition to the mission *ad gentes* ["to the nations"]; indeed, it has special links to that mission and is one of its expressions. This mission, in fact, is addressed to those who do not know Christ and his Gospel, and who belong for the most part to other religions.

In Christ, God calls all peoples to Himself and He wishes to share with them the fullness of His revelation and love. He does not fail to make Himself present in many ways, not only to individuals but also to entire peoples through their spiritual riches, of which their religions are the main and essential expression, even when they contain "gaps, insufficiencies and errors."[10] All of this has been given ample emphasis by the [Second Vatican] Council and the subsequent Magisterium, without detracting in any way from the fact that salvation comes from Christ and that dialogue does not dispense from evangelization.

In the light of the economy of salvation, the Church sees no conflict between proclaiming Christ and engaging in interreligious dialogue. Instead, she feels the need to link the two in the context of her mission *ad gentes*. These two elements must maintain both their intimate connection and their distinctiveness; therefore they should not be confused, manipulated, or regarded as identical, as though they were interchangeable.

I recently wrote to the bishops of Asia: "Although the Church gladly acknowledges whatever is true and holy in the religious traditions of Buddhism, Hinduism, and Islam as a reflection of that truth which enlightens all people, this does not lessen her duty and resolve to proclaim without fail Jesus Christ who is 'the Way, and the Truth, and the Life....' The fact that the followers of other religions can receive

God's grace and be saved by Christ apart from the ordinary means which He has established does not thereby cancel the call to faith and Baptism which God wills for all people."[11]

Indeed Christ Himself, "while expressly insisting on the need for faith and Baptism, at the same time confirmed the need for the Church, into which people enter through Baptism as through a door." Dialogue should be conducted and implemented with the conviction that the Church is the ordinary means of salvation and that she alone possesses the fullness of the means of salvation. [RM n. 55]

THE WEEK OF DECEMBER 5, 1999

49. DIALOGUE BASED ON RESPECT, HOPE, AND LOVE

[Inter-religious] dialogue does not originate from tactical concerns or self-interest, but is an activity with its own guiding principles, requirements, and dignity. It is demanded by deep respect for everything that has been brought about in human beings by the Spirit who blows where He wills. Through dialogue, the Church seeks to uncover the "seeds of the Word,"[12] a "ray of truth which enlightens all people"[13]; these are found in individuals and in the religious traditions of humanity.

Dialogue is based on hope and love, and will bear fruit in the Spirit. Other religions constitute a positive challenge for the Church: they stimulate her both to discover and acknowledge the signs of Christ's presence and the working of the Spirit, as well as to examine more deeply her own identity and to bear witness to the fullness of Revelation which she has received for the good of all.

This gives rise to the spirit which must enliven dialogue in the context of mission. Those engaged in this dialogue must be consistent with their own religious traditions and convictions, and be open to understanding those of the other party without pretense or close-mindedness, but with truth, humility, and frankness, knowing that dialogue can enrich each side. There must be no abandonment of principles nor false irenicism, but instead a witness given and received for mutual advancement on the road of religious inquiry and experience, and at the same time for the elimination of prejudice, intolerance, and misunderstandings. Dialogue leads to inner purification and conversion which, if pursued with docility to the Holy Spirit, will be spiritually fruitful. [RM n. 56]

WORKING FOR PEACE

"Blessed are the peacemakers," Jesus said; they have the high honor of being known as children of God, because they are fulfilling the desire of their heavenly Father (Mt 5:9).

THE WEEK OF DECEMBER 12, 1999

50. BUILDING PEACE

Precisely because of their faith, believers are called— as individuals and as a body—to be messengers and artisans of peace. Like others and even more than others, they are called to seek with humility and perseverance appropriate responses to the yearnings for security and freedom, solidarity and sharing, which are common to everyone in this world, which as it were has become smaller. A commitment to peace of course concerns every person of good will.... Yet this is a duty which is especially incumbent upon all who profess faith in God and even more so upon Christians, who have as their guide and master the "Prince of Peace" (Is 9:6)....

"Peace I leave with you; my peace I give to you," Christ has said to us (Jn 14:27). This divine promise fills us with the hope, indeed the certainty of divine hope, that peace is possible, because nothing is impossible with God (see Luke 1:37). For true peace is always God's gift, and for us Christians it is a precious gift of the risen Lord....

I wish to reaffirm the need for intense, humble, confident, and persevering prayer, if the world is finally to become a dwelling place of peace.

Prayer is *par excellence* the power needed to implore that peace and obtain it. It gives courage and support to all who love this good and desire to promote it in accordance with their own possibilities and in the various situations in which they live. Prayer not only opens us up to a meeting with the Most High but also disposes us to a meeting with our neighbor, helping us to establish with everyone, without discrimination, relationships of respect, understanding, esteem, and love....

Prayer is the bond which most effectively unites us. It is through prayer that believers meet one another at a level where inequalities, misunderstandings, bitterness, and hostility are overcome, namely before God, the Lord and Father of all. Prayer, as the authentic expression of a right relationship with God and with others, is already a positive contribution to peace. [TPS 37/3, 1992, 161-3, 166]

51. PEACE AND JUSTICE

Peace is a fundamental good which involves respecting and promoting essential human values: the right to life at every stage of its development; the right to be respected, regardless of race, sex, or religious convictions; the right to the material goods necessary for life; the right to work and to a fair distribution of its fruits for a well-ordered and harmonious coexistence. As individuals, as believers, and even more as Christians, we must feel the commitment to living these values of justice, which are crowned by the supreme law of love: "You shall love your neighbor as yourself" (Mt 22:39). [TPS 37/3, 1992, 164-5]

52. PEACE IS POSSIBLE

Peace is not a utopia, nor an inaccessible ideal, nor an unrealizable dream.

War is not an inevitable calamity.

Peace is possible.

And because it is possible, peace is our duty: our grave duty, our supreme responsibility.

Certainly peace is difficult; certainly it demands much good will, wisdom, and tenacity. But man can and he must make the force of reason prevail over the reasons of force.... And since peace, entrusted to the responsibility of men and women, remains even then a gift of God, it must also express itself in prayer to Him who holds the destinies of all peoples in His hands. [NE n. 13]

A FINAL WORD ON THE GREAT JUBILEE

I invite the faithful to raise to the Lord fervent prayers to obtain the light and assistance necessary for the preparation and celebration of the forthcoming Jubilee. I exhort my Venerable Brothers in the Episcopate and the ecclesial communities entrusted to them to open their hearts to the promptings of the Spirit. He will not fail to arouse enthusiasm and lead people to celebrate the Jubilee with renewed faith and generous participation.

I entrust this responsibility of the whole Church to the maternal intercession of Mary, Mother of the Redeemer. She, the Mother of Fairest Love, will be for Christians on the way to the Great Jubilee of the third millennium the star which safely guides their steps to the Lord. May the unassuming young woman of Nazareth, who two thousand years ago offered to the world the Incarnate Word, lead the men and women of the new millennium toward the One who is "the true light that enlightens every man" (Jn 1:9). [TMA n. 59]

As the Third Millennium Draws Near

(The complete official text of the apostolic letter
Tertio Millennio Adveniente *by His Holiness*
Pope John Paul II, released on November 14, 1994.)

To the Bishops, Priests and Deacons, Men and
Women Religious, and All the Lay Faithful

INTRODUCTION

1. As the third millennium of the new era draws near, our thoughts turn spontaneously to the words of the Apostle Paul, "When the fullness of time had come, God sent forth his Son, born of woman" (Gal 4:4). *The fullness of time coincides with the mystery of the Incarnation of the Word,* of the Son who is of one being with the Father, and with the mystery of the Redemption of the world. In this passage, St. Paul emphasizes that the Son of God was born of woman, born under the Law, and came into the world in order to redeem all who were under the Law so that they might receive adoption as sons and daughters. And he adds, "Because you are sons, God has sent the Spirit of his Son into our hearts, crying 'Abba! Father!'" His conclusion is truly comforting: "So through God you are no longer a slave but a son, and if a son then an heir" (Gal 4:6-7).

Paul's presentation of the mystery of the Incarnation contains *the Revelation of the mystery of the Trinity and the continuation of the Son's mission in the mission of the Holy Spirit.* The Incarnation of the Son of God, His conception and birth, is the prerequisite for the sending of the Holy Spirit. This text of St. Paul *thus allows the fullness of the mystery of the Redemptive Incarnation to shine forth.*

I
"JESUS CHRIST IS THE SAME YESTERDAY AND TODAY"
(Heb 13:8)

2. In his Gospel Luke has handed down to us a *concise narrative of the circumstances of Jesus' birth:* "In those days a decree went out from Caesar Augustus that all the world should be enrolled.... And all went to be enrolled, each to his own city. And Joseph also went up from Galilee, from the city of Nazareth, to Judea, to the city of David, which is called Bethlehem, because he was of the house and lineage of David, to be enrolled with Mary, his betrothed, who was with child. And while they were there, the time came for her to be delivered. And she gave birth to her first-born son and wrapped him in swaddling cloths, and laid him in a manger, because there was no place for them in the inn" (Lk 2:1, 3-7).

Thus was fulfilled what the Angel Gabriel foretold at the Annunciation, when he spoke to the Virgin of Nazareth in these words: "Hail, full of grace, the Lord is with you" (Lk 1:28). Mary was troubled by these words, and so the divine messenger quickly added: "Do not be afraid, Mary, for you have found favor with God. And behold, you will conceive in your womb and bear a son, and you shall call his name Jesus. He will be great and will be called the Son of the Most High.... The Holy Spirit will come upon you and the power of the Most High will overshadow you; therefore the child to be born will be called holy, the Son of God" (Lk 1:30-32, 35). Mary's reply to the angel was unhesitating: "Behold, I am the handmaid of the Lord; let it be to me according to your word" (Lk 1:38). Never in human history did so much depend, as it did then, upon the consent of one human creature.[1]

3. John, in the Prologue of his Gospel, captures in one phrase all the depth of the mystery of the Incarnation. He writes, *"And the Word became flesh and dwelt among us,* full of grace and truth; we have beheld his glory, glory as of the only Son from the Father" (1:14, RSV). For John, the Incarnation of the Eternal Word, of one being with the Father, took place in the conception and birth of Jesus. The Evangelist speaks of the Word who in the beginning was with God, and through whom everything which exists was made; the Word in whom was life, the life which was the light of men (cf. 1:1-4). Of the only-begotten Son, God from God, the Apostle Paul writes that He is *"the first-born of all creation"* (Col 1:15). God created the world through the Word. The Word is Eternal Wisdom; the Thought and Substantial Image of God; "He reflects the glory of God and bears the very stamp of his nature" (Heb 1:3). Eternally begotten and eternally loved by the Father, as God from God and Light from Light, he is the principle and archetype of everything created by God in time.

The fact that in the fullness of time the Eternal Word took on the condition of a creature gives a unique *cosmic value* to the event which took place in Bethlehem two thousand years ago. *Thanks to the Word, the world of creatures appears as a "cosmos,"* an ordered universe. And it is the same Word who, *by taking flesh, renews the cosmic order of creation.* The Letter to the Ephesians speaks of the purpose which God had set forth in Christ, "as a plan for the fulness of time, *to unite all things in him,* things in heaven and things on earth" (Eph 1:9-10).

4. Christ, the Redeemer of the world, *is the one Mediator between God and men,* and there is no other name under heaven by which we can be saved (cf. Acts 4:12). As we read in the Letter to the Ephesians: "In him we have redemption through his blood, the forgiveness of our trespasses, according to the richness of his grace, which he has lavished upon us. For he has made known to us in all wisdom and insight... his purpose which he set forth in Christ as a plan for the fulness of time, to unite all things in him, things in heaven and things on earth" (1:7-10). Christ, the Son who is of one being with the Father, is therefore the one who *reveals God's plan for all creation, and for man in particular.* In the memorable phrase of the Second Vatican Council, Christ "fully reveals man to man himself and makes his supreme calling clear."[2] He shows us this calling by revealing the mystery of the Father and His love. As the image of the invisible God, Christ is the perfect man who has restored to the children of Adam the divine likeness which had been deformed by sin. In His human nature, free from all sin and assumed into the divine Person of the Word, the nature shared by all human beings is raised to a sublime dignity: "By his incarnation the Son of God *united himself in some sense with every man.* He labored with human hands, thought with a human mind, acted with a human will and loved with a human heart. Born of Mary the Virgin he truly became one of us and, sin apart, was like us in every way."[3]

5. This "becoming one of us" on the part of the Son of God took place in the greatest humility, so it is no wonder that secular historians, caught up by more stirring events and by famous personages, first made only passing, albeit significant, references to Him. Such references to Christ are found for example in *The Antiquities of the Jews,* a work compiled in Rome between the years 93 and 94 by the historian Flavius Josephus,[4] and especially in the *Annals* of Tacitus, written between the years 115 and 120, where, reporting the burning of Rome in the year 64, falsely attributed by Nero to the Christians, the historian makes an explicit reference to Christ "executed by order of the procurator Pontius Pilate during the reign of Tiberius."[5] Suetonius, too, in his biography of the emperor Claudius, written around 121, informs us that the Jews were expelled from Rome because "under the instigation of a certain Chrestus they stirred up frequent riots."[6] This passage is generally interpreted as referring to Jesus Christ, who had become a source of contention within Jewish circles in Rome. Also of importance as proof of the rapid spread of Christianity is the testimony of Pliny the Younger, the Governor of Bithynia, who reported to the Emperor Trajan, between the years 111 and 113, that a large number of people were accustomed to gather "on a designated day, before dawn, to sing in alternating choirs a hymn to Christ as to a God."[7]

But the great event which non-Christian historians

merely mention in passing takes on its full significance in the writings of the New Testament. These
writings, although documents of faith, are no less
reliable as historical testimonies, if we consider their
references as a whole. Christ, true God and true
man, the Lord of the cosmos, is also the Lord of history, of which He is "the Alpha and the Omega" (Rv
1:8; 21:6), "the beginning and the end" (Rv 21:6). In
Him the Father has spoken the definitive word about
mankind and its history. This is expressed in a concise and powerful way by the Letter to the Hebrews:
"In many and various ways God spoke of old to our
fathers by the prophets; *but in these last days he has spoken to us by a Son"* (1:1-2).

6. Jesus was born of the Chosen People, in fulfillment of the promise made to Abraham and con-
stantly recalled by the Prophets. The latter spoke in
God's name and in his place. The economy of the
Old Testament, in fact, was essentially ordered to
preparing and proclaiming the coming of Christ, the
Redeemer of the universe, and of his Messianic
Kingdom. The books of the Old Covenant are thus a
permanent witness to a careful divine pedagogy.[8] *In
Christ* this pedagogy achieves its purpose: Jesus does
not in fact merely speak in the name of God like the
Prophets, but he is God Himself speaking in His
Eternal Word made flesh. Here we touch upon *the
essential point by which Christianity differs from all the
other religions,* by which *man's search for God* has been
expressed from earliest times. Christianity has its
starting point in the Incarnation of the Word. Here
it is not simply a case of man seeking God, but of

God who comes in Person to speak to man of Himself and to show him the path by which He may be reached. This is what is proclaimed in the Prologue of John's Gospel: "No one has ever seen God; the only Son, who is in the bosom of the Father, he has made him known" (1:18). *The Incarnate Word is thus the fulfillment of the yearning present in all the religions of mankind:* This fulfillment is brought about by God Himself and transcends all human expectations. It is the mystery of grace.

In Christ, religion is no longer a "blind search for God" (cf. Acts 17:27) but the *response of faith* to God who reveals Himself. It is a response in which man speaks to God as his Creator and Father, a response made possible by that one Man who is also the consubstantial Word in whom God speaks to each individual person and by whom each individual person is enabled to respond to God. What is more, in this Man all creation responds to God. Jesus Christ is the new beginning of everything. In Him all things come into their own; they are taken up and given back to the Creator from whom they first came. *Christ is thus the fulfillment of the yearning of all the world's religions and, as such, He is their sole and definitive completion.* Just as God in Christ speaks to humanity of Himself, so in Christ all humanity and the whole of creation speaks of itself to God—indeed, it gives itself to God. Everything thus returns to its origin. *Jesus Christ is the recapitulation of everything* (cf. Eph 1:10) and at the same time the fulfillment of all things in God: a fulfillment which is the glory of God. The religion founded upon Jesus Christ is a *religion of glory;* it is a newness of life for the praise of the glory of God (cf. Eph 1:12). All creation is in reality a manifestation of His glory. In particular, man (*vivens homo*) is the epiphany of God's glory, man who is called to live by the fullness of life in God.

7. *In Jesus Christ* God not only speaks to man but also *seeks him out.* The Incarnation of the Son of God attests that God goes in search of man. Jesus speaks of this search as the finding of a lost sheep (cf. Lk 15:1-7). It is a search which *begins in the heart of God* and culminates in the Incarnation of the Word. If God goes in search of man, created in His own image and likeness, He does so because He loves him eternally in the Word and wishes to raise him in Christ to the dignity of an adoptive son. God therefore goes in search of man who *is His special possession* in a way unlike any other creature. Man is God's possession by virtue of a choice made in love: God seeks man out, moved by His fatherly heart.

Why does God seek man out? Because man has turned away from Him, hiding himself as Adam did among the trees of the Garden of Eden (cf. Gn 3:8-10). *Man allowed himself to be led astray* by the enemy of God (cf. Gn 3:13). Satan deceived man, persuading him that he too was a god, that he, like God, was capable of knowing good and evil, ruling the world according to his own will without having to take into account the divine will (cf. Gn 3:5). Going in search of man through His Son, God wishes to persuade man to abandon the paths of evil which lead him farther and farther afield. "Making him abandon" those paths means making man understand that he is taking the wrong path; it means *overcoming the evil* which is everywhere found in human history. *Overcoming evil: this is the meaning of the Redemption.* This is brought about in the sacrifice of Christ, by which man redeems the debt of sin and is reconciled to God. The Son of God became man, taking a body and soul in the womb of the Virgin, precisely for this reason: to become the perfect redeeming sacrifice. The religion of the Incarnation is the *religion* of the world's Redemption through the sacrifice of Christ, wherein lies victory over evil, over sin, and over death itself. Accepting death on the Cross, Christ at the same time reveals and gives life because He rises again and death no longer has power over Him.

8. The religion which originates in the mystery of the Redemptive Incarnation is the religion of *"dwelling in the heart of God,"* of sharing in God's very life. St. Paul speaks of this in the passage already quoted: "God has sent the Spirit of his Son into our hearts, crying, 'Abba! Father!'" (Gal 4:6). Man cries out like Christ himself, who turned to God "with loud cries and tears" (Heb 5:7), especially in Gethsemane and on the Cross: man cries out to God just as Christ cried out to Him, and thus he bears witness that he shares in Christ's sonship through the power of the Holy Spirit. The Holy Spirit, whom the Father has sent in the name of the Son, enables man to share in the inmost life of God. He also enables man *to be a son, in the likeness of Christ,* and an heir of all that belongs to the Son (cf. Gal 4:7). In this consists the religion of "dwelling in the inmost life of God," which begins with the Incarnation of the Son of God. The Holy Spirit, who searches the depths of

God (cf. 1 Cor 2:10), leads us, all mankind, into these depths by virtue of the sacrifice of Christ.

II
THE JUBILEE OF THE YEAR 2000

9. Speaking of the birth of the Son of God, St. Paul places this event in the "fullness of time" (cf. Gal 4:4). *Time is indeed fulfilled by the very fact that God, in the Incarnation, came down into human history.* Eternity entered into time: what "fulfillment" could be greater than this? What other "fulfillment" would be possible? Some have thought in terms of certain *mysterious cosmic cycles* in which the history of the universe, and of mankind in particular, would constantly repeat itself. True, man rises from the earth and returns to it (cf. Gen 3:19): this is an immediately evident fact. Yet in man there is an irrepressible longing to live forever. How are we to imagine a life beyond death? Some have considered various forms of *reincarnation:* depending on one's previous life, one would receive a new life in either a higher or lower form until full purification is attained. This belief, deeply rooted in some Eastern religions, itself indicates that man rebels against the finality of death. He is convinced that his nature is essentially spiritual and immortal.

Christian Revelation excludes reincarnation, and speaks of a fulfillment which man is called to achieve in the course of a single earthly existence. Man achieves this fulfillment of his destiny through the sincere gift of self, a gift which is made possible only through his encounter with God. It is in God that man finds his full self-realization: *this is the truth revealed by Christ.* Man fulfills himself in God, who comes to meet him through his Eternal Son. Thanks to God's coming on earth, human time, which began at Creation, has reached its fullness. "The fullness of time" is in fact eternity, indeed, it is *the One who is eternal,* God Himself. Thus, to enter into "the fullness of time" means to reach the end of time and to transcend its limits, in order to find time's fulfillment in the eternity of God.

10. *In Christianity time has a fundamental importance.* Within the dimension of time the world was created; within it the history of salvation unfolds, finding its culmination in the "fullness of time" of the Incarnation and its goal in the glorious return of the Son of God at the end of time. *In Jesus Christ, the Word made flesh, time becomes a dimension of God,* who is Himself eternal. With the coming of Christ there begin "the last days" (cf. Heb 1:2), the "last hour" (cf. 1 Jn 2:18), and the time of the Church, which will last until the Parousia.

From this relationship of God with time there arises *the duty to sanctify time.* This is done, for example, when individual times, days, or weeks are dedicated to God, as once happened in the religion of the Old Covenant, and as happens still, though in a new way, in Christianity. In the liturgy of the Easter Vigil the celebrant, as he blesses the candle which symbolizes the risen Christ, proclaims: "Christ yesterday and today, the beginning and the end, Alpha and Omega, all time belongs to him, and all the ages, to him be glory and power through every age for ever."

He says these words as he inscribes on the candle the numerals of the current year. The meaning of this rite is clear: It emphasizes the fact that *Christ is the Lord of time;* He is its beginning and its end; every year, every day, and every moment are embraced by his Incarnation and Resurrection, and thus become part of the "fullness of time." For this reason, the Church too lives and celebrates the liturgy in the span of a year. *The solar year is thus permeated by the liturgical year,* which in a certain way reproduces the whole mystery of the Incarnation and Redemption, beginning from the first Sunday of Advent and ending on the Solemnity of Christ the King, Lord of the Universe and Lord of History. Every Sunday commemorates the day of the Lord's Resurrection.

11. Against this background we can understand *the Custom of Jubilees,* which began in the Old Testament and continues in the history of the Church. Jesus of Nazareth, going back one day to the *synagogue of his hometown,* stood up to read (cf. Lk 4:16-30). Taking the book of the Prophet Isaiah, he read this passage: "The Spirit of the Lord God is upon me, because the Lord has anointed me to bring good tidings to the afflicted; he has sent me to bind up the brokenhearted, to proclaim liberty to the captives, and the opening of the prison to those who are bound; *to proclaim the year of the Lord's favor"* (61:1-2).

The Prophet was speaking of the Messiah. "Today," Jesus added, "this scripture has been fulfilled in your hearing" (Lk 4:21), thus indicating that He Himself was the Messiah foretold by the prophet, and that the long-expected "time" was beginning in

Him. The day of salvation had come, the "fullness of time." *All Jubilees point to this "time" and refer to the Messianic mission of Christ,* who came as the one "anointed" by the Holy Spirit, the one "sent by the Father." It is He who proclaims the good news to the poor. It is He who brings liberty to those deprived of it, who frees the oppressed and gives back sight to the blind (cf. Mt 11:4-5; Lk 7:22). In this way He ushers in "a year of the Lord's favor," which He proclaims not only with His words but above all by His actions. The Jubilee, "a year of the Lord's favor," characterizes all the activity of Jesus; it is not merely the recurrence of an anniversary in time.

12. *The words and deeds of Jesus thus represent the fulfillment of the whole tradition of Jubilees* in the Old Testament. We know that the Jubilee was *a time dedicated in a special way to God.* It fell every seventh year, according to the Law of Moses: this was the "sabbatical year," during which the earth was left fallow and slaves were set free. The duty to free slaves was regulated by detailed prescriptions contained in the Books of Exodus (23:10-11), Leviticus (25:1-28), and Deuteronomy (15:1-6). In other words, these prescriptions are found in practically the whole of biblical legislation, which is thus marked by this very specific characteristic. In the sabbatical year, in addition to the freeing of slaves the Law also provided for the cancellation of all debts in accordance with precise regulations. And all this was to be done in honor of God. What was true for the sabbatical year was also true for the *Jubilee* year, which fell every fifty years. In the jubilee year, however, the customs of the sabbatical year were broadened and celebrated with even greater solemnity. As we read in Leviticus: "You shall hallow the 50th year and proclaim liberty throughout the land to all its inhabitants; it shall be a jubilee for you, when each of you shall return to his property and each of you shall return to his family" (25:10). One of the most significant consequences of the Jubilee year was the general *"emancipation" of all the dwellers on the land in need of being freed*. On this occasion every Israelite regained possession of his ancestral land, if he happened to have sold it or lost it by falling into slavery. He could never be completely deprived of the land, because it belonged to God; nor could the Israelites remain forever in a state of slavery, since God had "redeemed" them for Himself as His exclusive possession by freeing them from slavery in Egypt.

13. The prescriptions for the Jubilee year largely remained ideals—more a hope than an actual fact. They thus became a *prophetia futuri* insofar as they foretold the freedom which would be won by the coming Messiah. Even so, on the basis of the juridical norms contained in these prescriptions a kind of *social doctrine* began to emerge, which would then more clearly develop beginning with the New Testament. *The Jubilee year was meant to restore equality among all the children of Israel,* offering new possibilities to families which had lost their property and even their personal freedom. On the other hand, the Jubilee year was a reminder to the rich that a time would come when their Israelite slaves would once again become their equals and would be able to reclaim their rights. At the times prescribed by Law, a Jubilee year had to be proclaimed, to assist those in need. This was required by just government. *Justice, according to the Law of Israel, consisted above all in the protection of the weak,* and a king was supposed to be outstanding in this regard, as the psalmist says: "He delivers the needy when he calls, the poor and him who has no helper. He has pity on the weak and the needy, and saves the lives of the needy" (Ps 72:12-13). *The foundations of this tradition were strictly theological,* linked first of all with the theology of Creation and with that of Divine Providence. It was a common conviction, in fact, that *to God alone, as Creator, belonged the "dominium altum"*—lordship over all creation and over the earth in particular (cf. Lv 25:23). If in His Providence God had given the earth to humanity, that meant that He had given it to everyone. Therefore *the riches of Creation were to be considered as a common good of the whole of humanity.* Those who possessed these goods as personal property were really only stewards, ministers charged with working in the name of God, who remains the sole owner in the full sense, since it is God's will that created goods should serve everyone in a just way. *The Jubilee year was meant to restore this social justice.* The social doctrine of the Church, which has always been a part of Church teaching and which has developed greatly in the last century, particularly after the encyclical *Rerum Novarum,* is rooted in the tradition of the Jubilee year.

14. What needs to be emphasized, however, is what Isaiah expresses in the words "*to proclaim the year of the Lord's favor.*" For the Church, the Jubilee is precisely this "year of the Lord's favor," a year of the remission of sins and of the punishments due to them, a year of reconciliation between disputing parties, a year of manifold conversions and of sacramental and extra-sacramental penance. The tradition of Jubilee years involves the *granting* of indulgences on a larger scale than at other times. Together with Jubilees recalling the mystery of the Incarnation, at intervals of one hundred, fifty, and twenty-five years, there are also Jubilees which commemorate the event of the Redemption: the Cross of Christ, his death on Golgotha, and the Resurrection. On these occasions, the Church proclaims "a year of the Lord's favor," and she tries to ensure that all the faithful can benefit from this grace. *That is why Jubilees are celebrated not only "in Urbe" but also "extra Urbem":* traditionally the latter took place the year after the celebration "in Urbe."

15. *In the lives of individuals, Jubilees* are usually connected with the date of birth; but other anniversaries are also celebrated such as those of Baptism, Confirmation, First Communion, Priestly or Episcopal Ordination, and the Sacrament of Marriage. Some of these anniversaries have parallels in the secular world, but Christians always give them a religious character. In fact, in the Christian view every Jubilee—the 25th of Marriage or Priesthood, known as "silver," the 50th, known as "golden," or the 60th, known as "diamond"—is a *particular year of favor* for the individual who has received one or other of the Sacraments. What we have said about individuals with regard to Jubilees can also be applied to *communities* *or institutions.* Thus we celebrate the centenary or the millennium of the foundation of a town or city. In the Church, we celebrate the Jubilees of parishes and dioceses. All these personal and community Jubilees have an important and significant role in the lives of individuals and communities.

In view of this, *the two thousand years which have passed since the birth of Christ* (prescinding from the question of its precise chronology) *represent an extraordinarily great Jubilee,* not only for Christians but indirectly for the whole of humanity, given the prominent role played by Christianity during these two millennia. It is significant that the calculation of the passing years begins almost everywhere with the year of Christ's coming into the world, which is thus *the center* of the calendar most widely used today. Is this not another sign of the unparalleled effect of the birth of Jesus of Nazareth on the history of mankind?

16. *The term "Jubilee" speaks of joy;* not just an inner joy but a jubilation which is manifested outwardly, for the coming of God is also an outward, visible, audible, and tangible event, as St. John makes clear (cf. 1 Jn 1:1). It is thus appropriate that every sign of joy at this coming should have its own outward expression. This will demonstrate that *the Church rejoices in salvation.* She invites everyone to rejoice, and she tries to create conditions to ensure that the power of salvation may be shared by all. Hence the Year 2000 will be celebrated as the Great Jubilee.

With regard to its *content, this Great Jubilee* will be, in a certain sense, like any other. But at the same time it will be different, greater than any other. For the Church respects the measurements of time: hours, days, years, centuries. She thus goes forward with every individual, helping everyone to realize how *each of these measurements of time is imbued with the presence of God* and with His saving activity. In this spirit the Church rejoices, gives thanks, and asks forgiveness, presenting her petitions to the Lord of history and of human consciences.

Among the most fervent petitions which the Church makes to the Lord during this important time, as the eve of the new millennium approaches, is that unity among all Christians of the various confessions will increase until they reach full communion. I pray that the Jubilee will be a promising opportunity for fruitful cooperation in the many areas which unite us; these are unquestionably more numerous than those which divide us. It would thus be quite helpful if, with due respect for the programs of the individual churches and communities, ecumenical agreements could be reached with regard to the preparation and celebration of the Jubilee. In this way the Jubilee will bear witness even more forcefully before the world that the disciples of Christ are fully resolved to reach full unity as soon as possible in the certainty that "nothing is impossible with God."

III
PREPARATION FOR THE GREAT JUBILEE

17. *In the Church's history every Jubilee is prepared for by Divine Providence.* This is true also of the Great Jubilee of the Year 2000. With this conviction, we look today with a sense of gratitude and yet with a sense of responsibility at all that has happened in human history since the birth of Christ, particularly the events which have occurred between the years 1000 and 2000. But in a very particular way, we look with the eyes of faith to our own century, searching out whatever bears witness not only to man's history but also to God's intervention in human affairs.

18. From this point of view we can affirm that *the Second Vatican Council was a providential event whereby the Church began the more immediate preparation* for the Jubilee of the second millennium. It was a Council similar to earlier ones, yet very different; it was a Council *focused on the mystery of Christ and his Church, and at the same time open to the world.* This openness was an evangelical response to recent changes in the world, including the profoundly disturbing experiences of the twentieth century, a century scarred by the First and Second World Wars, by the experience of concentration camps, and by horrendous massacres. All these events demonstrate most vividly that the world needs purification; it needs to be converted.

The Second Vatican Council is often considered as the beginning of a new era in the life of the Church. This is true, but at the same time it is difficult to overlook the fact that *the Council drew much from the experiences and reflections of the immediate past,* especially from the intellectual legacy left by Pius XII. In the history of the Church, the "old" and the "new" are always closely interwoven. The "new" grows out of the "old," and the "old" finds a fuller expression in the "new." Thus it was for the Second Vatican Council and for the activity of the popes connected with the Council, starting with John XXIII, continuing with Paul VI and John Paul I, up to the present pope.

What these popes have accomplished during and since the Council, in their Magisterium no less than in their pastoral activity, has certainly made a significant contribution to the *preparation of that new springtime of Christian life* which will be revealed by the Great Jubilee, if Christians are docile to the action of the Holy Spirit.

19. The Council, while not imitating the sternness of John the Baptist, who called for repentance and conversion on the banks of the Jordan (cf. Lk 3:1-7), did show something of the Prophet of old, pointing out with fresh vigor to the men and women of today that Jesus Christ is the "Lamb of God who takes away the sin of the world" (Jn 1:29), the Redeemer of humanity, and the Lord of history. During the Council, precisely out of a desire to be fully faithful to her Master, the Church questioned herself about her own identity and discovered anew the depth of her mystery as the Body and the Bride of Christ. Humbly heeding the Word of God, she reaffirmed the universal call to holiness; she made provision for the reform of the liturgy, the "origin and summit" of her life; she gave impetus to the renewal of many aspects of her life at the universal level and in the local churches; she strove to promote the various Christian vocations, from those of the laity to those of religious, from the ministry of deacons to that of priests and bishops; and in a particular way she rediscovered episcopal collegiality, that privileged expression of the pastoral service carried out by the bishops in communion with the successor of Peter. On the basis of this profound renewal, the Council opened itself to Christians of other denominations, to the followers of other religions, and to all the people of our time. No council had ever spoken so clearly about Christian unity, about dialogue with non-Christian religions, about the specific meaning of the Old Covenant and of Israel, about the dignity of each person's conscience, about the principle of religious liberty, about the different cultural traditions within which the Church carries out her missionary mandate, and about the means of social communication.

20. The Council's enormously rich body of teaching and *the striking new tone* in the way it presented this content constitute as it were a proclamation of new times. The Council Fathers spoke in the language of the Gospel, the language of the Sermon on the Mount and the Beatitudes. In the Council's message God is presented *in his absolute lordship over all things,* but also as *the One who ensures the authentic autonomy of earthly realities.*

The best preparation for the new millennium, therefore, can only be expressed in a renewed commitment *to apply,* as faithfully as possible, *the teachings of Vatican II to the life of every individual and of the whole Church.* It was with the Second Vatican Council that, in the broadest sense of the term, the immediate preparations for the Great Jubilee of the Year 2000 were really begun. If we look for an analogy in the liturgy, it could be said that the yearly *Advent liturgy* is the season nearest to the spirit of the Council. For

Advent prepares us to meet the One who was, who is, and who is to come (cf. Rv 4:8).

21. Part of the preparation for the approach of the year 2000 is the *series of Synods* begun after the Second Vatican Council: general Synods together with continental, regional, national and diocesan Synods. The theme underlying them all is *evangelization,* or rather the new evangelization, the foundations of which were laid down in the Apostolic Exhortation *Evangelii Nuntiandi* of Pope Paul VI, issued in 1975 following the Third General Assembly of the Synod of Bishops. These Synods themselves are part of the new evangelization: they were born of the Second Vatican Council's vision of the Church. They open up broad areas for the participation of the laity, whose specific responsibilities in the Church they define. They are an expression of the strength which Christ has given to the entire People of God, making it a sharer in His own Messianic mission as Prophet, Priest, and King. Very eloquent in this regard are the statements of the Dogmatic Constitution *Lumen Gentium. The preparation for the Jubilee year 2000 is thus taking place throughout the whole Church, on the universal and local levels,* giving her a new awareness of the salvific mission she has received from Christ. This awareness is particularly evident in the Post-Synodal Exhortations devoted to the mission of the laity, the formation of priests, catechesis, the family, the value of penance and reconciliation in the life of the Church and of humanity in general, as well as in the forthcoming one to be devoted to the consecrated life.

22. Special tasks and responsibilities with regard to the Great Jubilee of the year 2000 belong to the *ministry of the Bishop of Rome*. In a certain sense, all the popes of the past century have prepared for this Jubilee. With his program to renew all things in Christ, St. Pius X tried to forestall the tragic developments which arose from the international situation at the beginning of this century. The Church was aware of her duty to act decisively to promote and defend the basic values of peace and justice in the face of contrary tendencies in our time. The Popes of the period before the Council acted with firm commitment, each in his own way: Benedict XV found himself faced with the tragedy of the First World War; Pius XI had to contend with the threats of totalitarian systems or systems which did not respect human freedom in Germany, in Russia, in Italy, in Spain, and even earlier still in Mexico. Pius XII took steps to counter the very grave injustice brought about by a total contempt for human dignity at the time of the Second World War. He also provided enlightened guidelines for the birth of a new world order after the fall of the previous political systems.

Furthermore, in the course of this century the Popes, following in the footsteps of Leo XIII, systematically developed the themes of Catholic social doctrine, expounding the characteristics of a *just system* in the area of relations between labor and capital. We may recall the encyclical *Quadragesimo Anno* of Pius XI, the numerous interventions of Pius XII, the encyclicals *Mater et Magistra* and *Pacem in Terris* of John XXIII, the Encyclical *Populorum Progressio* and the apostolic letter *Octogesima Adveniens* of Paul VI. I too have frequently dealt with this subject. I specifically devoted the encyclical *Laborem Exercens* to the importance of human labor, while in *Centesimus Annus* I wished to reaffirm the relevance, one hundred years later, of the doctrine presented in *Rerum Novarum*. In my encyclical *Sollicitudo Rei Socialis* I had earlier offered a systematic reformulation of the Church's entire social doctrine against the background of the East-West confrontation and the danger of nuclear war. The two elements of the Church's social doctrine—the *safeguarding of human dignity and rights* in the sphere of a just relation between labor and capital, and *the promotion of peace*—were closely joined in this text. The papal messages of 1 January each year, begun in 1968 in the pontificate of Paul VI, are also meant to serve the cause of peace.

23. Since the publication of the very first document of my Pontificate, *I have spoken explicitly of the Great Jubilee,* suggesting that the time leading up to it be lived as "a new Advent."[9] This theme has since reappeared many times, and was dwelt upon at length in the encyclical *Dominum et Vivificantem.*[10] In fact, preparing for the *year 2000 has become as it were a hermeneutical key of my Pontificate.* It is certainly not a matter of indulging in a new millenarianism, as occurred in some quarters at the end of the first millennium; rather, it is *aimed at an increased sensitivity to all that the Spirit is saying to the Church and to the churches* (cf. Rv 2:7 ff.), as well as to individuals through charisms meant to serve the whole community. The purpose is to emphasize what the Spirit is suggesting to the different communities, from the smallest ones, such as the family, to the largest ones, such as nations and international organizations, taking into account cultures, societies, and sound traditions. Despite appearances, humanity continues to await the revelation of the children of God and lives by this hope, like a mother in labor, to use the image employed so powerfully by St. Paul in his Letter to the Romans (cf. 8:19-22).

24. *Papal journeys* have become an important element in the work of implementing the Second Vatican Council. Begun by John XXIII on the eve of the Council with a memorable pilgrimage to Loreto and Assisi (1962), they notably increased under Paul VI, who after first visiting the Holy Land (1964) undertook nine other great apostolic journeys which brought him into direct contact with the peoples of the different continents.

The current Pontificate has widened this program of travels even further, starting with Mexico, on the occasion of the Third General Conference of the Latin American Episcopate held in Puebla in 1979. In that same year there was also the trip to Poland for the Jubilee of the nine hundredth anniversary of the death of St. Stanislaus, bishop and martyr.

The successive stages of these travels are well known. Papal journeys have become a regular occurrence, taking in the particular churches in every continent and showing concern *for the development of ecumenical relationships* with Christians of various denominations. Particularly important in this regard were the visits to Turkey (1979), Germany (1980), England, Scotland, and Wales (1982),

Switzerland (1984), the Scandinavian countries (1989), and most recently the Baltic countries (1993).

At present, it is my fervent wish to visit Sarajevo in Bosnia-Herzegovina and the Middle East: Lebanon, Jerusalem, and the Holy Land. It would be very significant if in the year 2000 it were possible to visit the *places on the road taken by the People of God of the Old Covenant*, starting from the places associated with Abraham and Moses, through Egypt and Mount Sinai, as far as Damascus, the city which witnessed the conversion of St. Paul.

25. In preparing for the year 2000, *the individual churches* have their own role to play, as they celebrate with their own Jubilees significant stages in the salvation history of the various peoples. Among these regional or *local Jubilees,* events of great importance have included the millennium of the Baptism of Rus' in 1988[11] as also the five hundredth anniversary of the beginning of evangelization in America (1492). Besides events of such wide-ranging impact, we may recall others which, although not of universal importance, are no less significant: for example, the millennium of the Baptism of Poland in 1966 and of the Baptism of Hungary in 1968, together with the six hundredth anniversary of the Baptism of Lithuania in 1987. There will soon also be celebrated the fifteen hundredth anniversary of the baptism of Clovis (496), King of the Franks, and the fourteen hundredth anniversary of the arrival of St. Augustine in Canterbury (597), marking the beginning of the evangelization of the Anglo-Saxon world.

As far as Asia is concerned, the Jubilee will remind

us of the Apostle Thomas, who, according to tradition, brought the proclamation of the Gospel at the very beginning of the Christian era to India, where missionaries from Portugal would not arrive until about the year 1500. The current year also marks the seventh centenary of the evangelization of China (1294), and we are preparing to commemorate the spread of missionary work in the Philippines with the erection of the Metropolitan See of Manila (1595). We likewise look forward to the fourth centenary of the first martyrs in Japan (1597).

In Africa, where the first proclamation of the Gospel also dates back to apostolic times, together with the 1,650th anniversary of the episcopal consecration of the first bishop of the Ethiopians, St. Frumentius (c. 340), and the five hundredth anniversary of the beginning of the evangelization of Angola in the ancient Kingdom of the Congo (1491), nations such as Cameroon, Côte d'Ivoire, the Central African Republic, Burundi and Burkina Faso are celebrating the centenaries of the arrival of the first missionaries in their respective territories. Other African nations have recently celebrated such centenaries.

And how can we fail to mention the Eastern Churches, whose ancient Patriarchates are so closely linked to the apostolic heritage and whose venerable theological, liturgical, and spiritual traditions constitute a tremendous wealth which is the common patrimony of the whole of Christianity? The many Jubilee celebrations in these churches and in the communities which acknowledge them as the origin of their own apostolicity recall the journey of Christ down the centuries, leading to the Great Jubilee at the end of the second millennium.

Seen in this light, the whole of Christian history appears to us as a single river, into which many tributaries pour their waters. The year 2000 invites us to gather with renewed fidelity and ever deeper communion *along the banks of this great river:* the river of Revelation, of Christianity, and of the Church, a river which flows through human history starting from the event which took place at Nazareth and then at Bethlehem two thousand years ago. This is truly the "river" which with its "streams," in the expression of the psalm, "make glad the city of God" (46:4).

26. The *Holy Years* celebrated in the latter part of this century have also prepared for the year 2000. *The Holy Year* proclaimed by Paul VI in *1975* is still fresh in our memory. The celebration of *1983* as *the Year of Redemption* followed along the same lines. *The Marian Year 1986/87* perhaps struck a more resounding chord; it was eagerly awaited and profoundly experienced in the individual local churches, especially at the Marian shrines around the world. The encyclical *Redemptoris Mater,* issued on that occasion, drew attention to the Council's teaching on the presence of the Mother of God in the mystery of Christ and the Church: two thousand years ago the Son of God was made man by the power of the Holy Spirit and was born of the Immaculate Virgin Mary. *The Marian Year was as it were an anticipation of the Jubilee,* and contained much of what will find fuller expression in the year 2000.

27. It would be difficult not to recall that the Marian Year took place only shortly before *the events of 1989.* Those events remain surprising for their vastness and especially for the speed with which they occurred. The '80s were years marked by a growing danger from the "Cold War." 1989 ushered in a peaceful resolution which took the form, as it were, of an "organic" development. In the light of this fact, we are led to recognize a truly prophetic significance in the encyclical *Rerum Novarum:* everything that Pope Leo XIII wrote there about Communism was borne out by these events, as I emphasized in the encyclical *Centesimus Annus.*[12] In the unfolding of those events one could already discern the invisible hand of Providence at work with maternal care: "Can a woman forget her infant?" (cf. Is 49:15).

After 1989 however there arose *new dangers and threats.* In the countries of the former Eastern bloc, after the fall of Communism, there appeared the serious threat of exaggerated nationalism, as is evident from events in the Balkans and other neighboring areas. This obliges the European nations to make a serious *examination of conscience* and to acknowledge faults and errors, both economic and political, resulting from imperialist policies carried out in the previous and present centuries vis-à-vis nations whose rights have been systematically violated.

28. In the wake of the Marian Year, we are now observing *the Year of the Family,* a celebration which is closely connected with the mystery of the Incarnation and with the very history of humanity. Thus there is good cause to hope that the Year of the

Family, inaugurated at Nazareth, will become, like the Marian Year, *another significant stage in preparation for the Great Jubilee.*

With this in view, I wrote a *Letter to Families,* the purpose of which was to restate the substance of the Church's teaching on the family and to bring this teaching, so to speak, into every home. At the Second Vatican Council, the Church recognized her duty to promote the dignity of marriage and the family.[13] The Year of the Family is meant to help make the Council's teaching in this regard a reality. *Each family, in some way, should be involved in the preparation for the Great Jubilee.* Was it not through a family, the family of Nazareth, that the Son of God chose to enter into human history?

IV
IMMEDIATE PREPARATION

29. Against the background of this sweeping panorama a question arises: Can we draw up *a specific program* of initiatives for the *immediate preparation* of the Great Jubilee? In fact, what has been said above already includes some elements of such a program.

A more detailed plan of specific events will call for widespread consultation in order for it not to be artificial and difficult to implement in the particular churches, which live in such different conditions. For this reason I wished to consult the Presidents of the Episcopal Conferences and especially the Cardinals.

I am grateful to the members of the College of Cardinals who met in Extraordinary Consistory on 13-14 June 1994, considered numerous proposals, and suggested helpful guidelines. I also thank my brothers in the Episcopate who in various ways communicated valuable ideas, which I have kept carefully in mind while writing this apostolic letter.

30. The first recommendation which clearly emerged from the consultation regards *the period of preparation*. Only a few years now separate us from the year 2000: it seemed fitting to divide this period into *two phases,* reserving the *strictly preparatory* phase for the last three years. It was thought that the accumulation of many activities over the course of a longer period of preparation would detract from its spiritual intensity.

It was therefore considered appropriate to approach the historic date with a *first phase,* which would make the faithful aware of general themes, and then to concentrate the direct and immediate preparation into a *second phase* consisting of a *three-year period* wholly directed to the celebration of the mystery of Christ the Savior.

A) First Phase

31. *The first phase* will therefore be of an *ante-preparatory* character; it is meant to revive in the Christian people an awareness of the value and meaning of the Jubilee of the year 2000 *in human history.* As a commemoration of the birth of Christ, the Jubilee is *deeply charged with Christological significance.*

In keeping with the unfolding of the Christian faith in word and sacrament, it seems important, even in this special anniversary, to link the structure of *memorial* with that of *celebration,* not limiting commemoration of the event only to ideas but also making its saving significance present through the celebration of the sacraments. The Jubilee celebration should confirm the Christians of today in their *faith* in God who has revealed himself in Christ, sustain their *hope* which reaches out in expectation of eternal life, and rekindle their *charity* in active service to their brothers and sisters.

During the first stage (1994 to 1996) the Holy See, through a special *Committee* established for this purpose, will suggest courses of reflection and action at the universal level. A similar commitment to promoting awareness will be carried out in a more detailed way by corresponding *commissions in the local churches.* In a way, it is a question of continuing what was done in the period of remote preparation and at the same time of *coming to a deeper appreciation of the most significant aspects of the Jubilee celebration.*

32. A Jubilee is always an occasion of special grace, "a day blessed by the Lord." As has already been noted, it is thus a time of joy. The Jubilee of the year 2000 is meant to be a great *prayer of praise and thanksgiving,* especially for the *gift of the Incarnation of the Son of God and of the Redemption* which He accomplished. In the Jubilee year Christians will stand with the renewed wonder of faith before the love of the Father, who *gave His Son,* "that whoever believes in him should not perish but have eternal life" (Jn 3:16). With a profound sense of commitment, they will likewise express their gratitude for the *gift of the Church,* established by Christ as "a kind of sacrament or sign of intimate union with God, and of the unity

140

of all mankind."[14] Their thanksgiving will embrace the *fruits of holiness* which have matured in the life of all those many men and women who in every generation and every period of history have fully welcomed the gift of Redemption.

Nevertheless, the joy of every Jubilee is above all a *joy based upon the forgiveness of sins, the joy of conversion.* It therefore seems appropriate to emphasize once more the theme of the *Synod of Bishops in 1984: penance and reconciliation.*[15] That synod was an event of extraordinary significance in the life of the postconciliar Church. It took up the ever topical question of conversion (*metanoia*), which is the precondition for reconciliation with God on the part of both individuals and communities.

33. Hence it is appropriate that, as the second millennium of Christianity draws to a close, the Church should become more fully conscious of the sinfulness of her children, recalling all those times in history when they departed from the spirit of Christ and his Gospel and, instead of offering to the world the witness of a life inspired by the values of faith, indulged in ways of thinking and acting which were truly *forms of counter-witness and scandal.*

Although she is holy because of her incorporation into Christ, the Church does not tire of doing penance: Before God and man *she always acknowledges as her own her sinful sons and daughters.* As *Lumen Gentium* affirms: "The Church, embracing sinners to her bosom, is at the same time holy and always in need of being purified, and incessantly pursues the path of penance and renewal."[16]

The Holy Door of the Jubilee of the year 2000 should be symbolically wider than those of previous Jubilees, because humanity, upon reaching this goal, will leave behind not just a century but a millennium. It is fitting that the Church should make this passage with a clear awareness of what has happened to her during the last ten centuries. She cannot cross the threshold of the new millennium without encouraging her children to purify themselves, through repentance, of past errors and instances of infidelity, inconsistency, and slowness to act. Acknowledging the weaknesses of the past is an act of honesty and courage which helps us to strengthen our faith, which alerts us to face today's temptations and challenges and prepares us to meet them.

34. Among the sins which require a greater commitment to repentance and conversion should certainly be counted those which *have been detrimental to the unity willed by God for His People.* In the course of the thousand years now drawing to a close, even more than in the first millennium, ecclesial communion has been painfully wounded, a fact "for which, at times, men of both sides were to blame."[17] Such wounds openly contradict the will of Christ and are a cause of scandal to the world.[18] These sins of the past unfortunately still burden us and remain ever present temptations. It is necessary to make amends for them, and earnestly to beseech Christ's forgiveness.

In these last years of the millennium, the Church should invoke the Holy Spirit with ever greater insistence, imploring from Him the grace of *Christian unity.* This is a crucial matter for our testimony to the

Gospel before the world. Especially since the Second Vatican Council many ecumenical initiatives have been undertaken with generosity and commitment: it can be said that the whole activity of the local churches and of the Apostolic See has taken on an ecumenical dimension in recent years. The *Pontifical Council for the Promotion of Christian Unity* has become an important catalyst in the movement toward full unity.

We are all however aware that the attainment of this goal cannot be the fruit of human efforts alone, vital though they are. *Unity, after all, is a gift of the Holy Spirit.* We are asked to respond to this gift responsibly, without compromise in our witness to the truth, generously implementing the guidelines laid down by the Council and in subsequent documents of the Holy See, which are also highly regarded by many Christians not in full communion with the Catholic Church.

This then is one of the tasks of Christians as we make our way to the year 2000. The approaching end of the second millennium demands of everyone an *examination of conscience* and the promotion of fitting ecumenical initiatives, so that we can celebrate the Great Jubilee, if not completely united, *at least much closer to overcoming the divisions of the second millen-nium.* As everyone recognizes, an enormous effort is needed in this regard. It is essential not only to continue along the path of dialogue on doctrinal matters, but above all to be more committed to *prayer for Christian unity.* Such prayer has become much more intense after the Council, but it must increase still more, involving an ever greater number of Christians, in unison with the great petition of Christ before his Passion: "Father... that they also may all be one in us" (cf. Jn 17:21).

35. Another painful chapter of history to which the sons and daughters of the Church must return with a spirit of repentance is that of the acquiescence given, especially in certain centuries, to *intolerance and even the use of violence* in the service of truth.

It is true that an accurate historical judgment cannot prescind from careful study of the cultural conditioning of the times, as a result of which many people may have held in good faith that an authentic witness to the truth could include suppressing the opinions of others or at least paying no attention to them. Many factors frequently converged to create assumptions which justified intolerance and fostered an emotional climate from which only great spirits, truly free and filled with God, were in some way able to break free. Yet the consideration of mitigating factors does not exonerate the Church from the obligation to express profound regret for the weaknesses of so many of her sons and daughters who sullied her face, preventing her from fully mirroring the image of her crucified Lord, the supreme witness of patient love and of humble meekness. From these painful moments of the past a lesson can be drawn for the future, leading all Christians to adhere fully to the sublime principle stated by the Council: "The truth cannot impose itself except by virtue of its own truth, as it wins over the mind with both gentleness and power."[19]

36. Many cardinals and bishops expressed the desire for a serious examination of conscience above all on the part of *the Church of today*. On the threshold of the new millennium Christians need to place themselves humbly before the Lord and examine themselves on *the responsibility which they too have for the evils of our day*. The present age in fact, together with much light, also presents not a few shadows.

How can we remain silent, for example, about the *religious indifference* which causes many people today to live as if God did not exist or to be content with a vague religiosity, incapable of coming to grips with the question of truth and the requirement of consistency? To this must also be added the widespread loss of the transcendent sense of human life and confusion in the ethical sphere, even about the fundamental values of respect for life and the family. The sons and daughters of the Church, too, need to examine themselves in this regard. To what extent have they been shaped by the climate of secularism and ethical relativism? And what responsibility do they bear, in view of the increasing lack of religion, for not having shown the true face of God, by having "failed in their religious, moral or social life"?[20]

It cannot be denied that for many Christians the spiritual life is passing through *a time of uncertainty* which affects not only their moral life but also their life of prayer and the *theological correctness of their faith*. Faith, already put to the test by the challenges of our times, is sometimes disoriented by erroneous theological views, the spread of which is abetted by the crisis of obedience vis-à-vis the Church's Magisterium.

And with respect to the Church of our time, how can we not lament *the lack of discernment,* which at times became even acquiescence, shown by many Christians concerning the violation of fundamental human rights by totalitarian regimes? And should we not also regret, among the shadows of our own day, the responsibility shared by so many Christians *for grave forms of injustice and exclusion?* It must be asked how many Christians really know and put into practice the principles of the Church's social doctrine.

An examination of conscience must also consider *the reception given to the Council,* this great gift of the Spirit to the Church at the end of the second millennium. To what extent has the Word of God become more fully the soul of theology and the inspiration of the whole of Christian living, as *Dei Verbum* sought? Is the liturgy lived as the "origin and summit" of ecclesial life, in accordance with the teaching of *Sacrosanctum Concilium?* In the universal Church and in the particular churches, is the ecclesiology of communion described in *Lumen Gentium* being strengthened? Does it leave room for charisms, ministries, and different forms of participation by the People of God, without adopting notions borrowed from democracy and sociology which do not reflect the Catholic vision of the Church and the authentic spirit of Vatican II? Another serious question is raised by the nature of relations between the Church and the world. The Council's guidelines—set forth in *Guadium et Spes* and other documents—of open, respectful, and cordial dialogue, yet accompanied by careful discernment and courageous witness to the truth, remain valid and call us to a greater commitment.

37. The Church of the first millennium was born of the blood of the martyrs: "*Sanguis martyrum—semen christianorum.*"[21] The historical events linked to the figure of Constantine the Great could never have ensured the development of the Church as it occurred during the first millennium if it had not been for the *seeds sown by the martyrs and the heritage of sanctity which marked the first Christian generations.* At the end of the second millennium, *the Church has once again become a Church of martyrs.* The persecutions of believers—priests, religious, and laity—has caused a great sowing of martyrdom in different parts of the world. The witness to Christ borne even to the shedding of blood has become a common inheritance of Catholics, Orthodox, Anglicans, and Protestants, as Pope Paul VI pointed out in his homily for the canonization of the Ugandan martyrs.[22]

This witness must not be forgotten. The Church of the first centuries, although facing considerable organizational difficulties, took care to write down in special martyrologies. Theses martyrologies have been constantly updated through the centuries, and the register of the saints and the blessed bears the names not only of those who have shed their blood for Christ but also of teachers of the faith, missionaries, confessors, bishops, priests, virgins, married couples, widows, and children.

In our own century the martyrs have returned, many of them nameless, *"unknown soldiers"* as it were *of God's great cause.* As far as possible, their witness should not be lost to the Church. As was recommended in the Consistory, *the local churches should do everything possible to ensure that the memory of those who have suffered martyrdom should be safeguarded, gathering the necessary documentation.* This gesture cannot fail to have an ecumenical character and expression. Perhaps the most convincing form of ecumenism is *the ecumenism of the saints* and of the martyrs. The *communio sanctorum* speaks louder than the things which divide us. The *martyrologium* of the first centuries was the basis of the veneration of the saints. By proclaiming and venerating the holiness of her sons and daughters, the Church gave supreme honor to God Himself; in the martyrs she venerated Christ, who was at the origin of their martyrdom and of their holiness. In later times there developed the practice of canonization, a practice which still continues in the Catholic Church and in the Orthodox Churches. In recent years the number of canonizations and beatifications has increased. These show *the vitality of the local churches,* which are much more numerous today than in the first centuries and in the first millennium. The greatest homage which all the churches can give to Christ on the threshold of the third millennium will be to manifest the Redeemer's all-powerful presence through the fruits of faith, hope, and charity present in men and women of many different tongues and races who have followed Christ in the various forms of the Christian vocation.

It will be the task of the Apostolic See, in preparation for the year 2000, *to update the martyrologies* for the universal Church, paying careful attention to the holiness of those who *in our own time* lived fully by the truth of Christ. In particular, there is a need to foster the recognition of the heroic virtues of men and women who have lived their Christian vocation *in marriage.* Precisely because we are convinced of the abundant fruits of holiness in the married state, we need to find the most appropriate means for discerning them and proposing them to the whole Church as a model and encouragement for other Christian spouses.

38. A further need emphasized by the cardinals and bishops is that of *continental synods,* following the example of those already held for Europe and Africa. The last General Conference of the Latin American Episcopate accepted, in agreement with the bishops of North America, the proposal for *a Synod for the Americas* on the problems of the new evangelization in both parts of the same continent, so different in origin and history, and on issues of justice and of international economic relations, in view of the enormous gap between North and South.

Another plan for a continent-wide synod will concern Asia, where the issue of the encounter of Christianity with ancient local cultures and religions is a pressing one. This is a great challenge for evangelization, since religious systems such as Buddhism or Hinduism have a clearly soteriological character. There is also an urgent need for a synod on the occasion of the Great Jubilee in order to illustrate and explain more fully the truth that Christ is the one Mediator between God and man and the sole Redeemer of the world, to be clearly distinguished from the founders of other great religions. With sincere esteem, the Church regards the elements of truth found in those religions as a reflection of the Truth which enlightens all men and women.[23] *"Ecce natus est nobis Salvator mundi*": In the year 2000 the proclamation of this truth should resound with renewed power.

Also for *Oceania* a regional synod could be useful. In this region there arises the question, among others, of the Aboriginal People, who in a unique way evoke aspects of human prehistory. In this synod a matter not to be overlooked, together with other problems of the region, would be the encounter of Christianity with the most ancient forms of religion, profoundly marked by a monotheistic orientation.

B) SECOND PHASE

39. On the basis of this vast program aimed at creating awareness, it will then be possible to begin the *second phase*, the strictly *preparatory* phase. This will take place *over the span of three years*, from 1997 to 1999. The thematic structure of this three-year period, *centered on Christ*, the Son of God made man, must necessarily be theological, and therefore *Trinitarian*.

YEAR ONE: JESUS CHRIST

40. *The first year*, 1997, will thus be devoted to *reflection on Christ*, the Word of God, made man by the power of the Holy Spirit. *The distinctly Christological character of the Jubilee* needs to be emphasized, for it will celebrate the Incarnation and coming into the world of the Son of God, the mystery of salvation for all mankind. The general theme proposed by many cardinals and bishops for this year is: "Jesus Christ, the one Savior of the world, yesterday, today, and for ever" (cf. Heb 13:8).

Among the Christological themes suggested in the Consistory the following stand out: a renewed appreciation of Christ, Savior and Proclaimer of the Gospel, with special reference to the fourth chapter of the Gospel of Luke, where the theme of Christ's mission of preaching the Good News and the theme of the Jubilee are interwoven; a deeper understanding of the mystery of the Incarnation and of Jesus' birth from the Virgin Mary; the necessity of faith in Christ for salvation. In order to recognize who Christ truly is, Christians, especially in the course of this year, *should turn with renewed interest to the Bible,* "whether it be through the liturgy, rich in the divine Word, or through devotional reading, or through instructions suitable for the purpose and other aids."[24] In the revealed text it is the Heavenly Father Himself who comes to us in love and who dwells with us, disclosing to us the nature of His only-begotten Son and His plan of salvation for humanity.[25]

41. The commitment, mentioned earlier, to make the mystery of salvation sacramentally present can lead, in the course of the year, to a *renewed appreciation of Baptism* as the basis of Christian living, according to the words of the Apostle: "As many of you as were baptized into Christ have put on Christ" (Gal 3:27). The *Catechism of the Catholic Church,* for its part, recalls that Baptism constitutes "the foundation of communion among all Christians, including those who are not yet in full communion with the Catholic Church."[26] From an *ecumenical point of view,* this will certainly be a very important year for Christians to look together to Christ the one Lord, deepening our commitment to become one in Him, in accordance with His prayer to the Father. This emphasis on the centrality of Christ, of the Word of God, and of faith ought to inspire interest among Christians of other denominations and meet with a favorable response from them.

42. Everything ought to focus on the primary objective of the Jubilee: the *strengthening of faith and of the witness of Christians.* It is therefore necessary to inspire in all the faithful *a true longing for holiness,* a deep desire for conversion and personal renewal in a context of ever more intense prayer and of solidarity with one's neighbor, especially the most needy.

The first year therefore will be the opportune moment for a renewed appreciation of *catechesis* in its original meaning as "the Apostles' teaching" (Acts 2:42) about the Person of Jesus Christ and His mystery of salvation. In this regard, a detailed study of the *Catechism of the Catholic Church* will prove of great benefit, for the catechism presents "faithfully and systematically... the teaching of Sacred Scripture, the living Tradition of the Church and the authentic Magisterium, as well as the spiritual heritage of the Fathers, doctors and saints of the Church, to allow for a better knowledge of the Christian mystery and for enlivening the faith of the People of God."[27] To be realistic, we need to enlighten the consciences of the faithful concerning errors regarding the Person of Christ, clarifying objections against Him and against the Church.

43. *The Blessed Virgin,* who will be as it were "indirectly" present in the whole preparatory phase, will be contemplated in this first year especially in the mystery of her divine motherhood. It was in her womb that the Word became flesh! The affirmation of the central place of Christ cannot therefore be separated from the recognition of the role played by his Most Holy Mother. Veneration of her, when properly understood, can in no way take away from "the dignity and efficacy of Christ the one Mediator."[28] Mary in fact constantly points to her Divine Son and she is proposed to all believers as the *model of faith* which is put into practice. "Devotedly meditating on her and contemplating her in the light of the Word made man, the Church with reverence enters more intimately into the supreme mystery of the Incarnation and becomes ever increasingly like her Spouse."[29]

YEAR TWO: THE HOLY SPIRIT

44. 1998, the *second year* of the preparatory phase, will be dedicated in a particular way to the *Holy Spirit* and to His sanctifying presence within the community of Christ's disciples. "The *great Jubilee* at the close of the second millennium...," I wrote in the encyclical *Dominum et Vivificantem,* "has a *pneumatological aspect* since the mystery of the Incarnation was accomplished 'by the power of the Holy Spirit.' It was 'brought about' by that Spirit—consubstantial with the Father and the Son—who, in the absolute mystery of the Triune God, is the Person-love, the uncreated gift, who is the eternal source of every gift that comes from God in the order of creation, the direct principle and, in a certain sense, the subject of God's self-communication in the order of grace. The *mystery of the Incarnation constitutes the climax* of this giving, this divine self-communication."[30]

The Church cannot prepare for the new millennium "in any other way than *in the Holy Spirit.* What was accomplished by the power of the Holy Spirit 'in the fullness of time' can only through the Spirit's power now emerge from the memory of the Church."[31]

The Spirit, in fact, makes present in the Church of every time and place the unique Revelation brought by Christ to humanity, making it alive and active in the soul of each individual: "The Counselor, the Holy Spirit, whom the Father will send in my name, he will teach you all things, and bring to your remembrance all that I have said to you" (Jn 14:26).

45. The primary tasks of the preparation for the Jubilee thus include *a renewed appreciation of the presence and activity of the Spirit,* who acts within the Church both in the sacraments, especially in *Confirmation,* and in the variety of charisms, roles, and ministries which He inspires for the good of the Church: "There is only one Spirit who, according to his own richness and the needs of the ministries, distributes his different gifts for the welfare of the Church (cf. 1 Cor 12:1-11). Among these gifts stands out the grace given to the Apostles. To their authority, the Spirit Himself subjected even those who were endowed with charisms (cf. 1 Cor 14). Giving the body unity through Himself and through His power and through the internal cohesion of its members, this same Spirit produces and urges love among the believers."[32]

In our own day too, the Spirit is *the principal agent of the new evangelization.* Hence it will be important to gain a renewed appreciation of the Spirit as the One who builds the Kingdom of God within the course of history and prepares its full manifestation in Jesus Christ, stirring people's hearts and quickening in our world the seeds of the full salvation which will come at the end of time.

46. In this *eschatological perspective,* believers should be called to a renewed appreciation of the theological virtue *of hope,* which they have already heard proclaimed "in the word of the truth, the Gospel" (Col 1:5). The basic attitude of hope, on the one hand, encourages the Christian not to lose sight of the final goal which gives meaning and value to life, and on the other, offers solid and profound reasons for a daily commitment to transform reality in order to make it correspond to God's plan.

As the Apostle Paul reminds us: "We know that the whole creation has been groaning in travail together until now; and not only the creation, but we ourselves, who have the first fruits of the Spirit, groan inwardly as we wait for adoption as sons, the redemption of our bodies. For in this hope we were saved" (Rom 8:22-24). Christians are called to prepare for the Great Jubilee of the beginning of the third millennium *by renewing their hope in the definitive coming of the Kingdom of God,* preparing for it daily in their hearts, in the Christian community to which they belong, in their particular social context, and in world history itself.

There is also need for a better appreciation and understanding of *the signs of hope present in the last part of this century,* even though they often remain hidden from our eyes. *In society in general,* such signs of hope include: scientific, technological, and especially medical progress in the service of human life, a greater awareness of our responsibility for the environment, efforts to restore peace and justice wherever they have been violated, a desire for reconciliation and solidarity among different peoples, particularly in the complex relationship between the North and the South of the world. *In the Church,* they include a greater attention to the voice of the Spirit through the acceptance of charisms and the promotion of the laity, a deeper commitment to the cause of Christian unity, and the increased interest in dialogue with other religions and with contemporary culture.

47. The reflection of the faithful in the second year of preparation ought to focus particularly *on the value of unity* within the Church, to which the various gifts and charisms bestowed upon her by the Spirit are directed. In this regard, it will be opportune to promote a deeper understanding of the ecclesiological doctrine of the Second Vatican Council as contained primarily in the Dogmatic Constitution *Lumen Gentium.* This important document has expressly emphasized that the unity of the Body of Christ *is founded on the activity of the Spirit,* guaranteed by the apostolic ministry and sustained by mutual love (cf. 1 Cor 13:1-8). This catechetical enrichment of the faith cannot fail to bring the members of the People of God to a more mature awareness of their own responsibilities, as well as to a more lively sense of the importance of ecclesial obedience.[33]

48. *Mary,* who conceived the Incarnate Word by the power of the Holy Spirit and then in the whole of her life allowed herself to be guided by His interior activity, will be contemplated and imitated during this year above all as the woman who was docile to the voice of the Spirit, a woman of silence and attentiveness, a woman of hope who, like Abraham, accepted God's will "hoping against hope" (cf. Rom 4:18). Mary gave full expression to the longing of the poor of Yahweh and is a radiant model for those who entrust themselves with all their hearts to the promises of God.

YEAR THREE: GOD THE FATHER

49. 1999, *the third and final year of preparation,* will be aimed at broadening the horizons of believers so that they will see things in the perspective of Christ: *in the perspective of the "Father who is in heaven"* (cf. Mt 5:45), from whom the Lord was sent and to whom He has returned (cf. Jn 16:28).

"This is eternal life, that they know you the only true God, and Jesus Christ whom you have sent" (cf. Jn 17:3). The whole of the Christian life is like a great *pilgrimage to the house of the Father,* whose unconditional love for every human creature, and in particular for the "prodigal son" (cf. Lk 15:11-32), we discover anew each day. This pilgrimage takes place in the heart of each person, extends to the believing community, and then reaches to the whole of humanity.

The Jubilee, centered on the person of Christ, thus becomes a great act of praise to the Father: "Blessed be the God and Father of our Lord Jesus Christ, who has blessed us in Christ with every spiritual blessing in the heavenly places, even as he chose us in him before the foundation of the world, that we should be holy and blameless before him" (Eph 1:3-4).

50. In this third year the sense of being on a journey to the Father should encourage everyone to undertake, by holding fast to Christ the Redeemer of man, a journey of authentic *conversion*. This includes both a "negative" aspect, that of liberation from sin, and a "positive" aspect, that of choosing good, accepting the ethical values expressed in the natural law, which is confirmed and deepened by the Gospel. This is the proper context for a renewed appreciation and more intense celebration of the *Sacrament of Penance* in its most profound meaning. The call to conversion as the indispensable condition of Christian love is particularly important in contemporary society, where the very foundations of an ethically correct vision of human existence often seem to have been lost.

It will therefore be necessary, especially during this year, to emphasize the theological virtue of *charity*, recalling the significant and lapidary words of the First Letter of John: "God is love" (4:8, 16). Charity, in its twofold reality as love of God and neighbor, is the summing up of the moral life of the believer. It has in God its source and its goal.

51. From this point of view, if we recall that Jesus came to "preach the good news to the poor" (cf. Mt 11:5; Lk 7:22), how can we fail to lay greater emphasis on the *Church's preferential option for the poor and the outcast?* Indeed,it has to be said that a commitment to justice and peace in a world like ours, marked by so many conflicts and intolerable social and economic inequalities, is a necessary condition for the preparation and celebration of the Jubilee. Thus, in the spirit of the Book of Leviticus (25:8-12), Christians will have to raise their voice on behalf of all the poor of the world, proposing the Jubilee as an appropriate time to give thought, among other things, to reducing substantially, if not canceling outright, the international debt which seriously threatens the future of many nations. The Jubilee can also offer an opportunity for reflecting on other challenges of our time, such as the difficulties of dialogue between different cultures and the problems connected with respect for women's rights and the promotion of the family and marriage.

52. Recalling that "Christ,... by the revelation of the mystery of the Father and his love, fully reveals man to man himself and makes his supreme calling clear,"[34] two commitments should characterize in a special way the third preparatory year: *meeting the challenge of secularism and dialogue with the great religions.*

With regard to the former, it will be fitting to broach the vast subject of the *crisis of civilization,* which has become apparent especially in the West, which is highly developed from the standpoint of technology but is interiorly impoverished by its tendency to forget God or to keep Him at a distance. This crisis of civilization must be countered by *the civilization of love*, founded on the universal values of peace, solidarity, justice, and liberty, which find their full attainment in Christ.

53. On the other hand, as far as the field of religious awareness is concerned, the eve of the year 2000 will provide a great opportunity, especially in view of the events of recent decades, for *interreligious dialogue*, in accordance with the specific guidelines set down by the Second Vatican Council in its declaration *Nostra Aetate* on the relationship of the Church to non-Christian religions.

In this dialogue the Jews and the Muslims ought to have a preeminent place. God grant that as a confirmation of these intentions it may also be possible to hold *joint meetings* in places of significance for the great monotheistic religions.

In this regard, attention is being given to finding ways of arranging historic meetings in places of exceptional symbolic importance like Bethlehem, Jerusalem, and Mount Sinai as a means of furthering dialogue with Jews and the followers of Islam, and to arranging similar meetings elsewhere with the leaders of the great world religions. However, care will always have [to] be taken not to cause harmful misunderstandings, avoiding the risk of syncretism and of a facile and deceptive irenicism.

54. In this broad perspective of commitments, *Mary Most Holy*, the highly favored daughter of the Father, will appear before the eyes of believers as the perfect model of love toward both God and neighbor. As she herself says in the canticle of the *Magnificat,* great things were done for her by the Almighty, whose name is holy (cf. Lk 1:49). The Father chose her for a *unique mission* in the history of salvation: that of being the Mother of the long-awaited Savior. The Virgin Mary responded to God's call with complete openness: "Behold, I am the handmaid of the Lord" (Lk 1:38). Her motherhood, which began in Nazareth and was lived most intensely in Jerusalem at the foot of the Cross, will be felt during this year as a loving and urgent invitation addressed to all the children of God so that they will return to the house of the Father when they hear her maternal voice: "Do whatever Christ tells you" (cf. Jn 2:5).

C) Approaching the Celebration

55. A separate chapter will be the *actual celebration of the Great Jubilee,* which will take place simultaneously in the Holy Land, in Rome, and in the local churches throughout the world. Especially in this phase, the *phase of celebration,* the aim will be *to give glory to the Trinity,* from whom everything in the world and in history comes and to whom everything returns. This mystery is the focus of the three years of immediate preparation: from Christ and through Christ, in the Holy Spirit, to the Father. In this sense the Jubilee celebration makes present in an anticipatory way the goal and fulfillment of the life of each Christian and of the whole Church in the Triune God.

But since Christ is the only way to the Father, in order to highlight His living and saving presence in the Church and the world, the *International Eucharistic Congress* will take place in Rome, on the occasion of the Great Jubilee. The year 2000 will be intensely eucharistic: in the *Sacrament of the Eucharist* the Savior, who took flesh in Mary's womb twenty centuries ago, continues to offer Himself to humanity as the source of divine life.

The ecumenical and universal character of the sacred Jubilee can be fittingly reflected by a *meeting of all Christians.* This would be an event of great significance, and so, in order to avoid misunderstandings, it should be properly presented and carefully prepared, in an attitude of fraternal cooperation with Christians of other denominations and traditions, as well as of grateful openness to those religions whose representatives might wish to acknowledge the joy shared by all the disciples of Christ.

One thing is certain: Everyone is asked to do as much as possible to ensure that the great challenge of the year 2000 is not overlooked, for this challenge certainly involves a special grace of the Lord for the Church and for the whole of humanity.

V
CONCLUSION

56. The Church has endured for two thousand years. Like the *mustard seed* in the Gospel, she has grown and become a great tree, able to cover the whole of humanity with her branches (cf. Mt 13:31-32). The Second Vatican Council, in its Dogmatic Constitution on the Church, thus addresses the question of *membership in the Church and the call of all people* *to belong to the People of God:* "All are called to be part of this Catholic unity of the new People of God.... And there belong to it or are related to it in various ways the Catholic faithful as well as all who believe in Christ, and indeed the whole of mankind, which by the grace of God is called to salvation."[35] Pope Paul VI, in the encyclical *Ecclesiam Suam,* illustrates how all mankind is involved in the plan of God and emphasizes the various circles of the dialogue of salvation.[36]

Continuing this approach, we can also appreciate more clearly the Gospel parable of the leaven (cf. Mt 13:33): Christ, like a divine leaven, always and ever more fully penetrates the life of humanity, spreading the work of salvation accomplished in the Paschal Mystery. What is more, He embraces within His redemptive power *the whole past history* of the human race, beginning with the first Adam.[37] The *future* also belongs to Him: "Jesus Christ is the same yesterday and today and for ever" (Heb 13:8). For her part the Church "seeks but a solitary goal: to carry forward the work of Christ himself under the lead of the Holy Spirit, the Paraclete. And Christ entered this world to give witness to the truth, to rescue and not to sit in judgment, to serve and not to be served."[38]

57. Therefore, ever since the apostolic age *the Church's mission* has continued without interruption within the whole human family. The first evangelization took place above all in the region of the Mediterranean. In the course of the first millennium, missions setting out from Rome and Constantinople brought Christianity to *the whole continent of Europe.* At the same time they made their way to the heart of *Asia,* as far as India and China. The end of the fifteenth century marked both the discovery of *America* and the beginning of the evangelization of those great continents, North and South. Simultaneously, while the sub-Saharan coasts of Africa welcomed the light of Christ, St. Francis Xavier, Patron of the Missions, reached Japan. At the end of the eighteenth century and the beginning of the nineteenth, a layman, Andrew Kim, brought Christianity to Korea. In the same period the proclamation of the Gospel reached Indochina, as well as *Australia and the islands of the Pacific.*

The nineteenth century witnessed vast missionary activity among the *peoples of Africa.* All these efforts bore fruit which has lasted up to the present day. The Second Vatican Council gives an account of this in the decree *Ad Gentes* on Missionary Activity. After the Council the question of missionary work was dealt with in the encyclical *Redemptoris Missio,* in the light of the problems of the missions in these final years of our century. In the future, too, the Church must continue to be missionary: Indeed missionary outreach is part of her very nature. With the fall of the great anti-Christian systems in Europe, first of Nazism and then of Communism, there is urgent need to bring once more the liberating message of the Gospel to the men and women of Europe.[39] Furthermore, as the encyclical *Redemptoris Missio* affirms, the modern world reflects the situation of the *Areopagus of Athens,* where St. Paul spoke.[40] Today there are many *"areopagi,"* and very different ones: These are the vast sectors of contemporary civilization and culture, of politics and economics. *The more the West is becoming estranged from its Christian roots, the more it is becoming missionary territory,* taking the form of many different "*areopagi.*"

58. The future of the world and the Church belongs to the *younger generation,* to those who born in this century will reach maturity in the next, the first century of the new millennium. *Christ expects great things from young people,* as He did from the young man who asked Him: "What good deed must I do, to have eternal life?" (Mt 19:16). I have referred to the remarkable answer which Jesus gave to him in the recent encyclical *Veritatis Splendor,* as I did earlier, in 1985, in my *Apostolic Letter to the Youth of the World.* Young people, in every situation, in every region of the world, do not cease to put questions to Christ: *They meet Him and they keep searching for Him in order to question Him further.* If they succeed in following the road which He points out to them, they will have the joy of making their own contribution to His presence in the next century and in the centuries to come, until the end of time: "Jesus is the same yesterday, today, and for ever."

59. In conclusion, it is helpful to recall the words of the Pastoral Constitution *Gaudium et Spes:* "The Church believes that Christ, who died and was raised up for all, can through his Spirit offer man the light and the strength to measure up to his supreme destiny. Nor has any other name under heaven been given to man by which it is fitting for him to be saved. She likewise holds that *in her most benign Lord and Master can be found the key, the focal point and the* *goal of all human history.* The Church also maintains that beneath all changes there are *so many realities which do not change and which have their ultimate founda-tion in Christ,* who is the same yesterday and today and forever. Hence in the light of Christ, the image of the unseen God, the firstborn of every creature, the Council wishes to speak to all men in order to illuminate the mystery of man and to cooperate in finding the solution to the outstanding problems of our time."[41]

While I invite the faithful to raise to the Lord fervent prayers to obtain the light and assistance necessary for the preparation and celebration of the forthcoming Jubilee, I exhort my venerable brothers in the Episcopate and the ecclesial communities entrusted to them to open their hearts to the promptings of the Spirit. He will not fail to arouse enthusiasm and lead people to celebrate the Jubilee with renewed faith and generous participation.

I entrust this responsibility of the whole Church to the maternal intercession of Mary, Mother of the Redeemer. She, the Mother of Fairest Love, will be for Christians on the way to the Great Jubilee of the third millennium the star which safely guides their steps to the Lord. May the unassuming young woman of Nazareth, who two thousand years ago offered to the world the Incarnate Word, lead the men and women of the new millennium toward the One who is "the true light that enlightens every man" (Jn 1:9).

With these sentiments I impart to all my Blessing.

From the Vatican, on 10 November in the year 1994, the seventeenth of my pontificate.

NOTES

1999
YEAR THREE OF PREPARATION
Returning to God the Father

1. St. Augustine, *In Iohannis Evangelium Tractatus*, 82, 3.
2. St. Augustine, *De Civitate Dei*, XIV, 28: *CCL* 48, p. 541.
3. John Paul II, Apostolic Exhortation *Reconciliatio et Paenitentia*, 18.
4. Vatican II, Pastoral Constitution on the Church in the Modern World *Gaudium et Spes*, 16.
5. *Gaudium et Spes*, 19.
6. *Lumen Gentium*, 11: *AAS* 57 (1965), 16.
7. Paul VI, Discourse to the Committee for the International Year of the Woman (April 18, 1975): *AAS* 67 (1975), 266.
8. John Paul II, Encyclical Letter *Sollicitudo Rei Socialis*, 34: *AAS* 80 (1988), 560.
9. *Gaudium et Spes*, 51.
10. Paul VI, *Address* at the Opening of the Second Session of the Second Vatican Ecumenical Council, September 29, 1963: *AAS* 55 (1963), 858.
11. Letter to the Fifth Plenary Assembly of Asian Bishops' Conferences (June 23, 1990), 4; *L'Osservatore Romano*, July 18, 1990.
12. Vatican II, Decree on the Missionary Activity of the Church *Ad Gentes*, 11, 15.
13. Vatican II, Declaration on the Church's Relations to Non-Christian Religions *Nostra Aetate*, 2.

As the Third Millennium Draws Near

1. Cf. Saint Bernard, *In Laudibus Virginis Matris, Homilia IV*, 8, *Opera Omnia*, Edit. Cister. (1966), 53.
2. *Gaudium et Spes*, 22.
3. *Gaudium et Spes*, 22.
4. Cf. *Ant. Iud.* 20:200, and the well-known and much-discussed passage in 18:63-64.
5. *Annales* 15:44, 3.
6. *Vita Claudii*, 25:4.
7. *Epist.* 10:96.
8. *Dei Verbum*, 15.

9. Encyclical Letter *Redemptor Hominis* (4 March 1979), 1: *AAS* 71 (1979), 258.

10. Cf. Encyclical Letter *Dominum et Vivificantem* (18 May 1986), 49ff.: *AAS* 79 (1986), 868ff.

11. Cf. Apostolic Letter *Euntes in Mundum* (25 January 1988): *AAS* 80 (1988), 935-56.

12. Cf. Encyclical Letter *Centesimus Annus* (1 May 1991), 12: *AAS* 83 (1991), 807-809.

13. *Gaudium et Spes*, 47-52.

14. *Lumen Gentium*, 1.

15. Cf. Apostolic Exhortation *Reconciliatio et Paenitentia* (2 December 1984): AAS 77 (1985), 185-275.

16. *Lumen Gentium*, 8.

17. *Unitatis Redintegratio*, 3.

18. *Unitatis Redintegratio*, 1.

19. Vatican II, Declaration on Religious Freedom *Dignitatis Humanae*, 1.

20. *Gaudium et Spes*, 19.

21. Tertullian, *Apol.*, 50:13: *CCL* 1:171.

22. Cf. *AAS* 56 (1964), 906.

23. *Nostra Aetate*, 2.

24. *Dei Verbum*, 25.

25. *Dei Verbum*, 2.

26. *Catechism of the Catholic Church*, No. 1271.

27. Apostolic Constitution *Fidei Depositum* (11 October 1992).

28. *Lumen Gentium*, 62.

29. *Lumen Gentium*, 65.

30. Encyclical Letter *Dominum et Vivificantem* (18 May 1986), 50: *AAS* 78 (1986), 869-870.

31. *Dominum et Vivificantem*, 51: *AAS* 78 (1986), 871.

32. *Lumen Gentium*, 7.

33. *Lumen Gentium*, 37.

34. *Gaudium et Spes*, 22.

35. *Lumen Gentium*, 13.

36. Cf. Paul VI, Encyclical Letter *Ecclesiam Suam* (6 August 1964), III: *AAS* 56 (1964), 650-657.

37. *Ecclesiam Suam*, 2.

38. *Gaudium et Spes*, 3.

39. Cf. Declaration of the Special Assembly for Europe of the Synod of Bishops, No. 3.

40. Cf. Encyclical *Redemptoris Missio* (7 December 1990), 37:AAS 83 (1991), 284-286.

41. *Gaudium et Spes*, 10.